CHURCH GIRL IS A GAY

A MEMOIR

For more information:
Stephen F. Austin State University Press
P.O. Box 13007 SFA Station
Nacogdoches, Texas 75962
sfapress@sfasu.edu
www.sfasu.edu/sfapress

Managing Editor: Kimberly Verhines
Book design: Katt Noble
Cover design: Kevin Ashburn

Distributed by Texas A&M Consortium
www.tamupress.com

ISBN: 978-1-62288-238-0

CHURCH GIRL IS A GAY

A MEMOIR

GINGER HENDRIX

STEPHEN F. AUSTIN STATE UNIVERSITY PRESS

FOR CHRISTI

CONTENTS

BEGINNING

PROLOGUE

The first concert I ever saw was at the Oral Roberts University Mabee Center. It was Sandee Pattie. Amy Grant was next up.

And the big praying hands painted to look like bronze were just a half block away, coming up out of the ground like there was a big brown man holding his breath underground below. I didn't know then that the best snowball fight of my life would happen around those hands on the vast, brown grass, snow-covered lawn in front of the medical center. All of us—the ones who seemed happy and the ones who didn't, the ones who never saw when they looked and the ones who seemed to always be searching, the scholarship kids and the ones forced to go—I bet 40 prep school kids in all, landed on that lawn just after it was hit with the first unslushy drop of the winter. And we picked up snow and threw it. And we laughed our asses off. It was like the grass below us was made of being 10 and we were covered in its permission all over again.

I was in love that day but I didn't know it then. And I can see her eyes flashing in the Oklahoma winter glare, easy in her claim of me and willing to watch me love her.

But I didn't know any of that then. I didn't know I loved her. Or the youth group girl before her or the camp counselor before her or even any of the women who seemed to throw a fishing line at my heart and lodge a hook that drug me to them.

It was 1985 and I was throwing snow inside the actual epicenter of American fundamentalism: in the center of the country, in the center of the southern midwest—those states without the ease of the south or the orderly Catholic goodness of the true midwest—in the center of the state proudest of the Bible, in the center of the city most in charge of declaring what that meant, in the center of the 320 evangelical charismatic acres that emanated its conviction out over the city like an ongoing firecracker of hot light. It was a city of answers to questions nobody even had a phone booth sized space of freedom to ask.

And I sure didn't. I was a church girl, a good one, the kind in the group who actually thought most of what we heard was a good idea. I didn't smoke in the parking lot or drink at the Quick Trip before Youth Group. ~~And I didn't kiss girls.~~

Not there, not in college later where I pogo-sticked from one evangelical set of acres to another, and not for all the years after where I lived and made all my decisions on a sort of evangelical party ship in the good company of people I'd found like me: too faithful to be Methodist but too smart to be Baptist and too committed to laughing to work inside actual churches.

We got back into our cars after that snowball fight in wet 501s and blasted the heater, and I blared Bruce Springsteen on my car radio and felt the pulsed beat of the real 80s rock that church music never could find.

I'd never been to a rock concert. I owned no vinyl. The cassette case I would finally buy myself three months later to take to college would be full of mixed tapes other people had made for me, and the names of bands who Casey Kasem knew. And I listened to all of it, but I sang the songs I'd lived inside: Vacation Bible School songs with hand motions and hymns and guitar-backed camp songs and soft 70s night-church choruses.

My soul didn't have its own radio then. It just played what it heard.

I took all my steps just above hard cement poured by Christians. On the linoleum of the church preschool and the shiny gray walkways of Sunday school hallways and the mopped floors of church kitchens, the dark pink carpets of sanctuaries, the flat black asphalt of church parking lots and the rocky concrete walkways of my evangelical liberal arts college and the wood planked decks I ran down laughing at camps all over the west. Even the driveway I stood in as I considered walking off every road I'd ever traveled was littered with the footprints of youth group leaders leading games out of my garage.

And it wasn't until my heart broke so badly that I couldn't stand up under the pain that my feet went looking for the soft, sandy ground of places where people weren't sure of most anything.

I was married with three kids, a leader in an evangelical non-profit. I was 48, and I knew my insides felt built to love a woman. But I still didn't know I was gay—because I'd never asked the question. There was no question available to ask.

END

GAY UNDERWEAR

The first thing I did when I came out to myself: I went and bought all new underwear. They needed to be more comfortable. I needed to not have to wear lady underwear anymore. Not that mine were covered in lace or anything, but there is this straight lady thing of buying the smallest size you can squeeze your ever-changing ass into. And there's always a size you hope to never have to buy. And I was over it.

I didn't go buy tight whites or anything, but I did get lady boxers— the sort of underwear any reasonable person would wear if they didn't feel like they had to look sexy. Mine had green stripes, were made of cotton and didn't seem to be wrestling against my backside.

I figured I couldn't go breaking the hearts of a field of people who I knew I'd disappoint while also picking my underwear out of my butt. "Son, I'm gay." *Yanks underwear out of crack.* "Honey, I love women." *Crack yank.* It also didn't look so good out ahead for meeting women: "Hey—I really like you. Wanna have dinner sometime?" *Dislodges Underpants with Straight Look on Face.* Buying new underwear felt like the right thing to do.

I figure now I've done most of the work of my coming out. What else could there be to pull off?

WHAT'S LEFT TO DO

Now all I have to do is tell my husband that I'm gay, and my three kids, and all of my church friends. And then talk to all of the people who will tell me how bad they feel for my husband and my kids. And the other people who will be trying to look at me lovingly but thinking "you queer mega-homo, lady-liking sinner bad person lezzie lez lez" And I'll have to not punch them. Or tell them to stick it. Or hit on them. And I still have to navigate my sons' responses and ready myself for their bitter betrayal and the way that my questioning my sexuality will make them stare at theirs just by virtue of possibility. And I have to ready myself for the day my daughter will be anywhere near old enough to navigate the same.

And I'll have to answer the question "Why?" and I won't know how to. "Why now? Why why? Why girls? Why did you wait so long? Why are you doing this to us? Why can't you just love Dad?" And I will have to say "I don't know. I don't know. I don't know. I don't know. And I do love your Dad. Very much. I love him enough to give him the chance to be adored. And it's not easy to let him go, actually. There's been a ration of intimacy I've been able to chew walking alongside your Dad. His soft eyes and his warm smile and his broad shoulders and the way he stands so quietly next to me when I'm with other people. But I needed to stop just not starving. I needed to pull up to a big table of comfort food and tuck in. And I needed for your Dad to be able to do that too. And it's just all harder than it looks. Trust me.

And he and I will remain friends, I promise. And we won't ever say a single bad thing about the other one. I'm going to make him swear to that. And I will carry the load of that commitment if I have to. And when he remarries, your new extra-woman-lady-extra-mom person will understand how it all works too. And she won't talk badly about me. Because I will have explained to her how our family works, and that there are requirements for adding yourself to it. And I will explain this to the women who I bring through the house door too—that loving you and Dad and whoever Dad loves is a requirement for loving me. That I'm not a separate package. And as awkward and weird as other people might think our family is, we are a family. We will be a family. We don't have to stop being a family because Dad and I don't stay connected in the same way. We can pick something different if we want. And that's what I want. And I think once Dad heals from his own deep-cut disappointment that he couldn't pull off what nobody could, he will be nodding alongside me to you, telling you that we will be a family. No matter what.

And I promise never to say 'I did this for you' or 'I needed to show you blah blah blah' Because I'm doing it for me. And you didn't have any control over it, not a bit. And whatever you learn from the way our family is going to shift will be yours, and I don't have a bit of say about what that will be.

All I have is the chance to feel comfortable in my own underpants that I can look right at you when you talk to me and, I hope too, when you don't.

CIGARETTE PRAYERS

Most days I drive myself to a particular little hill covered in ice plant that sits right above the beach near my house here on the central coast of California. I sit there and smoke cigarettes and tell God everything I think and wait for him to tell me back what he thinks. And the constant fog bank of my head tends to clear for moments there, gives me glimpses out to the possibility of days that might not look as bleak and heavy as these do, all of these days of heart break and risk and fuck-up—all this walking away from the good assurances of one life to hope myself to the arms of a another one I don't have the first idea will give me a thing.

I smoked my first cigarette in 17 years just about a month ago. I'd dropped the last half-used pack in the trash when my husband, then-boyfriend, found them in my glove box: "Are these yours?" Then I just threw them away. Threw away the sweet soft gin-rush of nicotine. And this was before I'd found gin, so it was a particularly sad thing to toss out: the one cigarette on the drive home from classes. Or the one on the wall at Butterfly Beach, while I sat sad and trying hard to find enough of a grappling hook inside me to hang on to my flat faith. The ones on the steps with my roommate, exhaling out the day. All those one-cigarette-at-a-times, gone.

So when I picked up the re-entry pack at a filling station on my way north to stay with a friend and pound out what was so wrong and lonely inside my marriage, I opened it and smoked the whole thing. Every. Last. Cigarette. And after my first inhale, that one long-awaited mega-drag, I let out a moaning cry like I hadn't in a long time. A sorrowful wail of yearning and finding. Made that same sound at the first drag of every cigarette in the pack. And I smelled like an ashtray when I landed at her house, didn't try to hide it with gum or spray. Just hugged her and said, "I smoked on the way here." She said "Oh." And that was all. And now more packs, more deep calm, more little bits of death to calm my soul, more nicotine to buzz out my sadness and worry. More feel in my mouth of sucking in something you want that nobody says you should have. "It'll kill ya," and you think *But I want it.*

I've started smoking while I drive around town now. And I'm barely using the botanical spray I've been covering myself up with these last weeks. Want to smell like smoke now, I think. Want some people around me to see me in my car with a cigarette hanging off my lip, cut straight to "She's a smoker?" Kind of like that tactic "Dad, I have a brain tumor. Just kidding, I'm gay." Feels like I want to smell like disappointing change, let everybody know what's coming in some small smelly way so they'll be more ready for what they have coming.

CHURCH GIRL

It will be impossible for some to believe me that I have not been hiding, lying about who I am, who I love. They will think I'm dodging the question, or that I'm too embarrassed to tell that much of the truth.

Maybe only former church kids will get it. Any of us who felt pulled to move close to a same-gendered person were just pointed away—the way you grab a kid who's heading into traffic and point them toward the sidewalk. Youth group leaders did this, parents did this, eventually we all did this for ourselves. It was like having a crossing guard inside your soul. Nope—not that way. Go over there.

We didn't know any gays. I mean, I'm sure we knew gobs, but in the 70's they weren't really hanging out at our church potlucks. At least not while telling anybody they were there, I guess. Nobody said they were real. Nobody said anything at all about them, actually. I'd say that homosexuality was poured into the general soup of debauchery. It was in there with alcohol and cigarettes and playing cards and people who wore really tight clothing. It was mixed in with a list of activities that would send you straight to hell, and—even more terrifying—right out the door.

Given the option, I would have chosen invisibility or maybe jumping over tall things as a God-given super power, but apparently mine is self-restriction. It isn't surprising, of course, because I was raised Nazarene—which is like being Catholic without the wine and all the cool relatives who swear. We didn't drink. We didn't dance. We didn't play cards.

We did have our own traditions too, but none with the deep history or generational connection of Yom Kippur or even No-Meat Fridays. They were things like Alabaster Sunday, when everybody paraded up the aisle to the front to dump the change they'd been saving for missionaries way far away—it was like an audible declaration of the amount of Christian you were, with the little tinkles telling everybody you were a selfish change-hoarding piece of non-Christian work and the loud crashes a declaration to the whole crowd of your self-restricting sacrifice for far-off strangers.

I remember those Sundays because of the way my parents ran all over the house scouring it for pennies and dimes before we left for church. And for the way I sat on their bed slump-shouldered and feeling like an alabaster failure.

And we had Wednesday Night Potlucks. Everybody came with Pyrex dishes full of goopy concoctions made out of some part of heaven. We would all sit at long foldable church tables with paper plates heaping with food on our plates, one cream of chicken soup casserole blending over into the next one, everyone spooning hoards of melted cheese and green Jell-O into their cake holes like a bunch of lushes. Gluttony wasn't on our list of seven deadly sins. They were more like:

1. Dancing
2. Drinking
3. Watching the movie "Grease"
4. Wearing non-one-piece suits in pools with boys
5. Sexish activities of all kinds
6. Forgetting to bring your Bible to Sunday School
7. Making bad potluck food

I was taught to be an expert in what not to do. No running in church. No talking. No taking off your shoes and sliding down the slick cemented hallways to the Sunday School rooms. No talking too much or too loud. No wearing pants. No raising your hand too many times when somebody is talking and you have something to add. No cutting in the potluck line.

And then later, no sex. Nobody had to say no sex with women. They were proud of their wildly abstaining heterosexuality, all those boys believed to be just at the edge of screwing us when we weren't looking. And my memories of all my time with friends away from adults after the age of about eleven was the thick sexual tension of a small group of us in a darkened corridor or a shut storage closet, surrounded by stacks of chairs, sidling up next to the thing we were sure must be great since they spent so much time telling us not to touch it.

So I guess I'm not surprised that I naturally restrict myself. I do it now without thinking.

I stopped listening to the Indigo Girls and Melissa Etheridge one day, I don't know when it was exactly, but it was a long time ago, and it didn't have anything to do with not loving their music. I did. I do. They play guitar the way I want to when I play—intimately and with, well authenticity balls. No watching the Ellen Show. No seeing a movie that might have a sister somewhere who's a lesbian. And no maintaining friendship with women who magnetized my heart. I never wrote these down. I never shared them or declared them in any way. I just kept crossing things off the list of possibility and turning my head in another direction.

I learned this tactic from my mother, who believed wholeheartedly in the power of proximity to influence us all unto deadly acts of sin. I couldn't watch Laverne and Shirley because they worked bottling beer. I'm pretty sure it wasn't even the constant Milwaukee-accented innuendo she was keeping me from. It was the beer she didn't want me to see rolling past on conveyor belts—believing somehow that the sight of it would give me a creeping taste for beer that I'd never otherwise find. And no playing with Barbie because she didn't wear underwear.

No crimes of proximity. No crimes of an accidental Yes.

THE PRAYER

I woke up a little worried I'm not gay this morning, couldn't drum up the normal series of fantasies that get me through the awake patches in the night. Can't decide to imagine who to be with. Have lost my head's partner, and so am looking in my mind for someone else to canoodle with. The celebrities all fell flat, too self-serious for me, too sure of their own deep sex-well for me to have anything to give. And all my friends are, well, my friends.

So I've found myself imagining a woman whose face I cannot yet see. Beginning to feel the hold of her, but no kisses, no mouth, no eyes, just a barely-coming closeness. And not enough to think about in the middle of the night. It is more of a daytime vision, a sitting-in-the-ice plant on a hill overlooking the sand and the water kind of thing. I see her sort of dimly as I build the prayer I'm building out to the beach heaven—

Dear God,
Can I please have a woman who will receive all I have to give and give back some of her own, who will be taken by me but can't be overtaken, who will tell me when I'm wrong, who will love my children even during the stretch of time they will not love her, who will remain unburdened and unafraid of the architecture of my particular soul.

SCRIBBLED MANIFESTO

I will not steal love. I will wait to have love offered and I will take it in whatever size it comes. Small kisses, long hugs, short ones. Real looks. Deeper love, all the sex that makes its way to me. I won't steal any. I won't talk anybody into anything or stand at the edges of possibilities, hopeful and wanting. I'll give and receive love only. From here on out.

HEY BUDDY

Feels like my soul's been a fucking lunatic for a few months, staggering around like a gin-soaked, love-struck 14 year old. Or, actually, I guess that was me, not my soul. But still my soul's been useless too, kicking off from the same piece of steel playground equipment, the kind that spins just above the dirt and delivers nothing but the pull of a spin, doesn't catapult you anywhere or swing you up to any new vantage point. Glad to be off that damn thing, jumped the dirt ruts left there by all those kids running to get it going, and I'm sitting on some bench now hoping the mild nausea doesn't send me puking into the park trash. And I guess that's an upgrade.

I see beautiful women everywhere now, the way when you buy a Prius you all of a sudden feel like everybody else is driving them now too. They're everywhere you look. And yes I just compared a beautiful woman to a car, which I regret.

I have had the thought this week, "Am I objectifying women?" That would be the best, weirdest, most unexpected move of my life: young feminist, once a 35-year old mom of two who wouldn't hesitate to flip off any dumb trucker with a playboy tire flap, even with the toddlers in the car, the only one of two of us in my college feminism class at our small Christian college in the 80's who didn't nod with assent at the curly-headed girl who stood up and said to the packed room of baseball players and other such numbnuts, "I just wanna be able to stay home and have kids."

Me: I might be objectifying women.

Staring at their breasts everywhere I go. Maybe I'll get to have a moment where some gorgeous woman looks at me all annoyed and says, "Hey, Buddy, eyes up here."

SEEING STRAIGHT

My friend whose wisdom I trust more than anyone's asked me yesterday to wait to ask the question "Am I gay?" until after Christmas. Until my chemistry falls in line. Until I can see straight. Until I can see clearly, she must have said. We have loved each other like sisters since my early twenties. I rocked all of her babies, joined in on most of her family vacations before I had my own, and have spent most of my adult years believing everything she's told me.

"Because of the kids," she said. "I don't think I can walk with you..." something something. It's a blur after that. Think she said something about not believing that an alternative lifestyle would fill the need I feel. And that it's a hazardous question because of my kids.

"I'll think about it," was all I could swing. And then my head shook itself because the question feels like it's asked me, and not me it. I've known—she's known—that I am attracted to many of the women I meet, that I am "same sex attracted" they would call it. I asked the question "Am I attracted to women?" years ago. But the only right answer to that one is "Better Not Be."

"It's a new question for me," I said.

"But you had that thing years ago—you've asked it before," she said.

"No I haven't," I said. This is a new question, about 10 days old.

ANOTHER PRAYER

Please stay my God, Please stay my God.
Give me a better ending than I can see.

DEAD LIFTING

"I haven't thought about being gay at all this morning," I wrote in my journal. Does it mean you're not gay enough to be gay if you don't always do everything gay-ly? gay-ish? Is gayness something that trumps all of your other somethings? Are you allowed to ask other questions while you're asking the question, "Am I gay?"—like "What am I going to make for dinner?" and "If my husband still seems cute to me, does that mean I'm not gay?" Because he does.

All his kindness is making his face sort of glow, and I like his sweet face. It is dear to me. *Your kindness to me, your kindness to me, what can death do.* Those lines come to me from the poem I wrote for ailing Ruth, as I picture him in the chair I finally found that's big enough for him—furniture he can't break—sitting up sort of straight and asking me about my appointment with the psychiatrist. "How are you?" I said after I'd told him all the details about the Wellbutrin and the Lexapro and the way she said, "You've been under-treated for a really long time.": "I just want to get this figured out," he said, and he tried to smile a little like he was nice while he said it, and he is nice while he says it, and also I know he must be so clenched inside, standing with the barbell in the high position of the dead weight lift, staying there, maneuvering too long during a time when you're supposed to just show off and then drop the weight.

LISA THE THERAPIST

"How gay do you have to be to be gay?"

This is the question I threw out at the beginning of my first session with Lisa the Therapist. She took a beat to answer, was checking, I think, to make sure I wasn't joking. And then she continued with a kind, "How do you mean?" And I told her everything.

"You said you are a part of the Christian community—how will this affect that?" She asked after I laid it all out.

"I don't have a spiritual crisis going, really," I said. "I think God is perfectly happy to have me as I am. I don't sense his despair or disapproval, think he wants to continue to have me. But I will lose 25-year friendships, I suspect. I will lose some for even asking the question at all, it's looking like." For years my participation in the community was so important to me that I didn't ask the question at all, I told her. If the answer was yes, it woulda been a no-go for me.

"They're telling me to stay and work it out with my husband," I said. "They're telling me it would be best to stay."

But some days I want to die, I told her—which is the only reason I'm asking myself the question *Am I gay?* in the first place. Asking it has been the only power-cutting source so far to stop what sounds in my head like the good idea of going away forever.

HOROSCOPES ARE BAD

I never let myself read horoscopes before. Always nervous, I guess, that it might be true. I read mine for the first time: "During the next two and a half days you may feel rather unlike yourself."

Also, I will only get along with Geminis and, since I don't know any Geminis besides me, this makes sense since I don't feel like being around anybody else.

My mother was dead afraid of horoscopes. She got a "that's a bad bad man" look on her face when the topic came up or somebody mentioned they'd read them…ever.

Horoscopes were up there with people who didn't believe in the Bible, anybody who thought you could get unsaved or who said you couldn't keep a gun at home, and blonde women. These were things to step around.

My mother's only two blonde friends rocked their roots regularly or got their frost on, so this must have given them a pass. Blonde women were maybe more to be feared than even horoscopes, as I think about it. My mother would cock her head to the side the way a curious dog might, and then sort of bulge her eyes cold and forward with a cheek smile only. Everything about her body said "Nope."

When a blonde woman grabbed my mother's man later, I'm sure it only sent hot glue straight from her soul to her face to cement that look. Something in her must have been nodding and telling herself that she always knew, that she'd been right to trust her fears because they never lied.

I wonder if the reason my mother didn't read horoscopes was that she was afraid they might be true. She wanted to protect her sources, never let herself find out that more things besides the bible and her own fears might make sense.

EYES DOWN

I have my eyes down now really everywhere I can, trying so hard to honor my husband and also to honor one pal's desperately sad and angry-eyed command to me: *I need you to stop.* Stop looking outside my marriage, stop living inside my alternate fantasy lesbian love universe, stop risking so much pain for my kids, stop hacking away at my husband's trust in me. She doesn't need me to stop asking the question, doesn't need me to guarantee any outcomes of the question I'm asking, just wants me to stop fucking around. And I heard her. And I'm trying to stop.

SECOND BAPTISM

I baptized myself. I have tried to push that word away, call what I did something else, but I know that is what I was doing when I walked to the edge of the ocean, stripped off my shorts and shirt and walked into the water in my bra and underwear.

I kept walking, through the small waves and then into the bigger ones, let them push me back and then I kept pushing forward at them. I got myself to the scariest place I could muster. Took a pummeling for a while. I imagine that I did dip under, which most would call baptism, but it was the wave-hit I walked in for—that water crash and the force and the asking for it again and enduring it and asking for it again. And there was a moment when I'd deemed I'd had enough, and so I walked back up to the shore and sat on my shorts in my underwear for a bit. I left something there in the ocean. Some portion of my longing, some stack of fantasy, the taste for a blast that would blow a big enough hole in my life for me to walk out of it.

It wasn't my first baptism. This time no one was watching. This time I was alone. This time it wasn't echoey. This time my best friend was not with me. This time her father did not hold our hands together and, one at a time, submerge us in chlorined water and pray a prayer over us. This time I did not walk back up slippery baptismal steps in drenched clothing behind the girl who all the boys loved. This time I dried off in the sun, in my underwear, with the sound of the waves still crashing.

FIRST LANGUAGE

We spoke Non-Verbal in the home. The way a person walks or the direction of their eye or the movement of their arms or whatever their hips are doing, or the tone and pitch and rapidity or sluggishness of their speech, the way they set their purse down and where, what they look away from—these are the messages that reach me naturally.

I hear them the way someone would hear their native French in a crowded English-speaking airport. They come into my ear like the things that happen after words land, they arrive like pure meaning, little chunks of data. I have never yet managed to turn this language off, no matter how many times I've been asked to or tried—it's always seemed to me that I was being asked to have an open garden hose pointed at my face but to not act spluttery or wet.

My mother could say "I am incredibly angry with the situation you've put me in with this person standing across from us" by shifting her sunglasses with her left hand from the side just a little higher onto her nose. My father could say "You fucking piss me off" by a clinch of his jaw.

I could tell how they were getting along from where I sat in the backseat, even in a silent car. The more beyond that is the stuff of the garden hose—all the messages I've translated for so long that they skip any conscious effort and arrive like message meaning. My brain works to hear nonverbal messages the way my knees do to drive my manual car, from muscle memory and repetition and from throwing the clutch enough times that I know when to concentrate and when to just let the messages come.

I was taught to pray in my second language. I want to love and be loved in my first.

WHAT WE SAID

My husband asked me a question one morning that I answered—can't remember what it was—and then he said, "Yeah, you'd said that" as he got up and walked to the door to keep at his morning routine. And then I saw him realize what he'd done, that he'd opened a door to me and quickly shut it.

He turned and came back and said, "But you can tell me again," and put a pillow at the other end of the bed and asked me more about my time with Lisa the Therapist, and I told him how all I'd really done so far was tell her stories, and he said, "That must have been hard."

And I said, Yeah, it made me tired."

And then he said, "I'll love you no matter what."

And I said that back to him. And we both really, really meant it. And it's a sentence I've carried in my pocket, a smooth stone to rub for comfort.

WHAT THE HIGH SCHOOL BF SAID

George Winston's *December* was on my No-Way-No-How list. Which is weird, because George Winston is not a lesbian as far as I know. But he does play the piano music that my best friend and I used to listen to while we laid on top of the covers of her bed on our backs and let ourselves cry about the way our broken-apart families were fucking up our hearts. About the way that we were the best grown-ups we knew, the way that all the older people had gone to hell and were useless to us.

I think I stopped letting myself listen to it because of all that sadness, and likely because some part of my soul knew I'd been in love with her during those years. And too the way it made me really feel what I was feeling.

And then these two messages arrived to my phone yesterday: "You've always had a deep current of unsettled waters humor doesn't fix." And "You've always been uncomfortable with your femininity."

Not my horoscope. A message from her, my high school best friend, the one who I lost for 15 years, who stopped returning my calls even after so many of them, the one who I finally noticed needed to be away, and so who I let leave. She reappeared last year, through a Facebook message and we picked up the jog of our friendship as if she'd sat down on a bench for a bit to gather her strength, and then we were running again. The way we did along the Arkansas River when we were roommates in '86—paced and coached by her, steadied and believed in, and then pushed at the last for a heaving sprint.

She told me about myself yesterday when I finally asked her, found myself texting her the words that had been sitting on a pad of paper in my mind for the past month. "Is there anything about me that you've always known?" And she sent the messages back to me one at a time, with sets of hours between them. "More thoughts to share when we're together." And reading those gave me a little tremble, the floor shake of something real and inevitable to hear from her. A believable soul telling a truth back, sent from thirty years ago and for me now.

LISA THE THERAPIST #2

I read my prayer aloud for the first time today, to Lisa the Therapist, struggled to begin the first words, *"Can I please have a woman…"* Finally read it through and immediately put my face straight into my hands.

"Shame," she said. "I see shame."

Yes, so much shame. "You're not supposed to love women," I said.

A MAN CALLED HORSE

I saw the movie *A Man Called Horse* when I was about nine. My uncle took me to the theater—must have been babysitting and really wanted to see it himself. It was a terrifyingly violent film, and I stayed in my seat as long as I could, didn't run down the aisle in the dark, heading for the exit door until the boy was hoisted by a rope hooked right into the flesh of his chest, pulleyed up by his tribe to prove he could survive the pain his coming manhood was going to bring, his muscles tensing to stay as still as he possibly could so the weight of the ascent wouldn't splay the wound and kill him as they raised him up.

And I can see myself swinging there, and I don't blame the tribe or the agreements we all made that living in this world means following the customs we're up to our necks in. I think I stepped up to the ropes just like he did, let them puncture me through and willed myself not to pass out or cry in front of the whole gang of them, told myself it would be over soon and put my head to staying still and enduring the pain of proving I was who they knew I was supposed to be.

CROSSING

I am not new to worry and fear. They've been two heavy suitcases I've dragged around for years, one in each hand, always having to be set down where no one would take them, then picked up and hauled again to my next landing spot. I have been the woman who overpacked for the weekend always, with cases full of things I don't need—a just in case sort of packer for life, ready with a cadre of self-protective skills on hand for any given emotional worst case scenario:

- Self-effacement in case of potential embarrassment;
- Defensiveness in case of soul-accurate attack;
- Deflection for dangerous proximity to vulnerable truths;

And fear, just general, spray-as-you-go fear, in an endlessly refilling case of aerosol bottles, always at the ready to be finely showered on the ground before me—for snakes, failure, men with darting eyes, enclosed spaces, the TSA, unlocked doors, and pants that don't hide my biggish ass.

I want to set them down, the cases, and move forward like walking rocks across a creek, just one at a time—reaching the first foot out and landing the other, waiting for steadiness before trying to proceed.

It is the beginning of a river cross for me. I can see the dry shore behind me, all those I love standing on the bank, feel the splash of water on my ankles and a different sort of mist—running water, uncaged and cool. And I hope some of those I love on the bank will follow me. And I hope I don't fall in. And I hope I don't turn back. And I hope I make it to the other side. And I hope I don't look back over my shoulder to calculate my coming losses.

I hope I wait to hear which foot follows on the rock behind me. I hope I will know whose it is just by the sound of the footfall and the sheer force of their approach.

MIDDLE

CLASSIC GOD

The waves hit softly, landing with the sound you use to keep babies sleeping, and I sit on the hill lulled by them, the waves nothing like the ones I threw myself into. No crashing.

A cigarette prayer: *Jesus, I love women.*

And incoming: *I know.* His hand to my head. His hand to the top of my head. I can see the words I wrote as a young poet, floating there on a scrap of paper: "Please touch the top of my head sometimes. If you are near me, and you think of it, just sort of rest your hand there on the place that was soft longer than the rest of my skull, where the skin used to dip and wrinkle." This sensation is the same, the slight weight of a hand, a blessing-giving hand.

And incoming: *Good job. . .* and then some silence and next: *Blessed are you among women.*

Wait, I said back. Didn't think I could say I'd heard the blessed virgin's words from Gabriel about my pulling off the trembling courage of telling the truth about myself. So I listened again. *Blessed are you among women.* And then I laughed hard—an unattractive bursting laugh: I am, in fact, God, blessed when I'm among women. Solid point. And then I laughed more and shook my head and smoked with slow drags and tried not to plan the coming days or years.

Lisa the Therapist asked me a question later I couldn't answer. I told her about the hilarity of the "Blessed are you among women" blessing and she said, "Do you think that could be about anything else?" And I didn't see it—the gift of the joke felt like enough for me, really. But I see what she was seeing now: Blessed are you among women, the angel Gabriel says to the girl, the girl who has just said yes to the unexpected and unknown road, who agrees to go trustingly, who puts her eyes on the voice inside her that says, "Yes, go" and away from the questions that had to have plagued her— her love or at least agreements with Joseph, the coming stares of her family and all of those people who didn't know her but who would weigh in with opinions about her obvious infraction. She saw the terror and uncertainty and stepped forward anyhow.

I'm no Virgin Mary, but I see it too. I am receiving blessings—the one from the incoming prayer, the way that my husband receives me and dares to love me, and the "I don't care if you're gay" reassurances from my pal who cares about every last part of me and made clear that none of that has changed a bit when I told her.

No one will believe me that when I got up from the ice plant, grabbed up my cigarettes and keys, then got into the car to go home and plugged in the music that had been running on my playlist while I smoked, that this is what I heard: my favorite part, that last spunked and riffy guitar solo from Diana's anthem, the one we all must capture when we do what I just did: "I'm Coming Out." And then I laughed again. Another loud one. Shook my head more. Why wouldn't God speak to me in irreverent whispers of his love for me, assure me of the way that I am seen? Classic God.

CIGARETTE PRAYERS #2

The far coastline was sparkly clear for the first time yesterday morning, and the dark bits of sand were skimming across the light ones. The day before, hawks were playing on the wind currents. My ice plant time has been quieter, more watchful. More sitting in a new steadiness these past couple of days. Taking in the way my gut has shifted from tight to loose and a portion of my achy sadness has lifted, feels less likely to pop my chest open, my prayers just varying versions of *Please* and *Thank You.*

I have been seeing the way that I've been a horse in central park for so many years: blinders on so I'd just get the job done of pulling the wagon. And I don't mean the wagon is my husband. I don't mean it's my kids or my years of loving and stretching inside of a beautiful evangelical Christian organization that wants kids to know Jesus. But I do mean I've been dragging a weight, some rock marked *you better not.*

Today's incoming cigarette prayer: *I love you. You're ok.* And mine outgoing, just some words of Patty Griffin's "Heavenly Day":

> No one at my shoulder bringing me fears.
> Got no clouds up above me bringing me tears.
> Got nothing to tell you, I've got nothing much to say.
> Only I'm glad to be here with you on this heavenly,
> Heavenly, heavenly, heavenly day.

BINGE WATCHING *THE FOSTERS*

I binge watched *The Fosters*. Eleven episodes, up until 3:30am. It is absolutely mid-life lesbian porn—all those freshly chopped salads mixed with kitchen kisses, the struggling teenagers growing in their emotional intelligence as they fuck up with drugs and sex and chores, all five of them well-fed and working out their conflicts with two women who are patient and real and whose craftsman style home I want to live in with those unbelievably gorgeous solid wood doors. And the kisses, I replayed them and replayed them. The kisses. Steamy in their hunger for closeness, playful, rolled into the bumpy mix of regular life.

I watched the way you eat a really good, big bowl of noodles—taking in more whole mouthfuls even after you're full, just wanting the taste and feel of it. Let myself look at the things I'd not let myself see. Some days it feels like feasting, and some days overeating from a buffet line. All that tenderness and all those eyes seeing each other. The couch kissing and the bed kissing and the after-fight kissing and the car kissing—and at the places they put their hands on one another, the hands on necks and on cheeks, down the deep lower back, and a hand laid gently to the high spot on our chests where we breathe. All that claiming and reclaiming with hands and mouths that lovers do when they lean in with their bodies for each other.

I have been a magnet trying to walk away from all the smallest shards of metal in the world. Never mind the steel beams of drawing encounters and the way they felt attached somewhere to the inside of that place that rests right below my heart, the honest place that tells me how I really feel.

GOALS

I have said that my parents' divorce wrecked me, undid me. But it was really the early years of carrying it alone, maneuvering through the shrapnel of it that tore me up. They limped and stormed away into their own respective sadness and anger, and I was left with the job of finding a life without either of them, a life I'd barely had in the few of my late adolescent years before they split. All of the outside of my life began to match the inside of it. All my aloneness became circumstantial, impossible to hide, not even from myself.

I think of my children having to duck and cover and maneuver in and because of this unrest, this explosion, this undoing of their lives. And so, these goals, clear and whole and firm come from some unmoving pillar inside of me:

1. I will stay with my children through whatever our lives serve up to us. I won't let them feel the hit of any of it alone.

2. I will make a space for them, a safe welcoming space, for all the years I know them. I won't make them stay in it. But I'll protect it for them.

3. I won't use the hits I take in life to escape from the responsibility of loving them well, from the charge that came with their births. I will stay nearby, as nearby as they'll let me stay. And I won't falter in walking next to them, at whatever distance or closeness they'll allow.

TELLING HIM

I told him.

And before I even had a chance to say "I am gay, honey—I love women," he said: "I don't want you to worry about hurting to me. I just want you to be honest."

And then I was, and then he said more things like, "I appreciate your being brave," and "You're not going to be alone." And we sat on the balcony on chairs and talked more and I cried, and it was as connective a time with my husband as I can remember—much like the sacred space of our moments in between long contractions at the end of hours and hours of labor, the quiet eye conversations of knowing, empathetic love.

There was his open posture, his quiet, his honesty and the way when he said, "What are we going to do?" he was beginning a conversation, not claiming an impossibility and also declaring a truth we share—that we don't know what we are going to do. And I sat with the way he said, "We will figure it out," more than once, and the way that I know he means it. And that figuring out won't include any more of my hiding or pushing down my desire to love a woman deeply and hungrily. And it won't involve our dumping our kids into some sad, conflicted, confused space between fighting ex-loves.

We have said so far that we will honor each other as we go forward, and that we'll get to share our kids together, just like we're sharing the ache and the relief of telling the truth that our love is shifting into the unknown.

MUSCLE MEMORY

I checked in with my husband and leaned in to kiss him without thinking, the muscle memory of marriage, and he leaned toward me and turned his cheek right to my lips just before they landed. And I remembered then where we are now. It's easy to forget, what with the way we are sharing the same bed like camp mates and trying to handle all this laundry and bill paying. And the way that it feels so easy between us finally, all that disappointment and pressure like a smelly pot we burned on the stove and set outside under the tree in the backyard to cool.

We talked later and he said, "I want a wife."

And this thought later on: *I want a wife too.*

CIGARETTE PRAYERS #3

The coastline is shrouded this morning. If I didn't know where I lived—a crook in the coast along the middle of California—I'd think it didn't exist. The wind isn't up this morning, so there's a wet haze all around. I sit on a chair to keep my butt from getting wet in the ice plant, have a few cigarettes, wait for any incoming prayers. Not much today. Just my outgoing: *I want to be held. I want to be held.* It's a plea more than a prayer, but most of my prayers seem to be, so I'll count it as real.

And yes, I count them, was taught to so early that it's hard to stop. Quiet times were on the list with Bible reading and scripture memory— extra points for remembering to bring your Bible, bring your friends, bring your right answers. Spiritual life then was like walking on a treadmill that they turned up the speed on every time you did something right. I force myself now to ignore whether or not I'm doing it all right because it's completely depressing to track spiritual failure the way they taught us to in Sunday School. These beach times have been the best most real prayers of my life, I think.

The warm wave of nicotine is the closest thing to the feeling of being held that I've found, some sort of inner release of tension and worry. That same feeling when you come out of the cold ocean and lie down on a towel to dry in the sun. For now, it will be lots and lots of cigarettes for me.

I've got a callous on my right thumb from the cigarette lighter. This has to be some sort of symbol of nicotine commitment, some way smokers secretly feel each other's hands to know if they're in the presence of another. This has come not only because I've been puffing cigarettes like my grandpa popped antacids—sort of constantly throughout the day with gaps in between for eating—but also because I smoke in the wind a lot, so my flick-to-light ratio is off. It'll take me 9 or 10 tries on the days when the wind is coming toward me off the water. I turn my body to block the wind and cup my hand around the cigarette and try and try. So I've got some burns too. And I'm sincerely hoping that this is the one single thing in my life that's not a metaphor.

SOUL RADIO

My soul has a sort of radio of its own, so I regularly hear myself humming something nobody's played on any actual radio within miles, a little offering of whatever my insides have been chewing on in the night, a missive of honesty. It's one of the ways I know what I'm feeling, since I am otherwise pretty thick at recognizing my own feeling state. My soul uses its radio to wave its arms at me. I've learned to stop and see what it's waving about.

This morning I sat in peace in the ice plant and watched the surfers fight the waves in the fog and listened to A Great Big World's "You'll Be Okay" playing on my soul's radio. So nice to know my insides see the way ahead.

GO BACK

Today I sat in my car and let the nicotine flood of my first cigarette wash over me. Nicotine on an empty stomach. So wonderful. "I would have been a good drug addict," I said out loud by myself in my car.

And then an incoming prayer: *Go back.* And an immediate outgoing: *Fuck.* And I could see the knife right there at my wrist, the picture of it in my head was right there. *I can't go back. I can't do that. So even though I have believed all of my incoming prayers, this one must not be real because I can't do that. I can't go back to my marriage.*

So I took myself out of my car and went to the ice plant and sat, and shook my head and muttered some things that I don't remember. And kept shaking my head. *I can't. Don't make me do this.* And then*: Just go back to him.* And then I got a little stillness. *I can do that.* Because I left again a day or two ago. It only takes that long for me to be gone from him completely, upstairs watching lesbians on television hold on to each other tearfully with a grip of connectedness I'm still waiting for. But I do need to go back to him. Need to keep walking with him. Need to go at his pace, which is infuriating because it's so goddamn slow and I'm so ready to run now.

But I can do this. And I will do this. I will stop living upstairs. I will go back to him. So we can walk shoulder to shoulder. And then I will likely need to do this coming back over and over again. Incoming: *Are we clear?* Outgoing: *Got it.*

I watched that lesbian show "The L Word" last night. Finished "The Fosters" and all their committed hand-holding love and was looking for another something to see. It was a bunch of women sitting around a table leering at other women across the room. Pairs and pairs of lesbians emotionally disconnected but talking constantly about fucking each other. I didn't like it. It's not what I want. I want heat, but not that kind, not the kind that is so hungry that it mows over all the women in front of it. I want the kind that arcs across two people. I want the loving kind of heat. And I wonder if this will take years to find, and then years to grow.

And I wonder if my body will even be in solid enough shape to really feel it. I wonder if I will let myself walk away from my marriage and then be alone waiting for love for a long long time. And I don't know any of the answers to what I wonder.

WHAT WE SAID #2

My husband and I sat on the balcony this weekend and had more tears together. "You are my chosen family," he said. "I don't want to lose you." We have built a family together with a handful of dear friends, which is what you do when your relatives are all dead or nuts or live really far away. And even in light of what we're looking at now, that way of living is rooted deep enough in us both to want to keep walking in it. Then we sort of sad-dreamed together about the way we would really love to go forward. Together.

Feels like my current life is gone. And I'm just figuring out what life looks like now that it is. And all of it is the sort of thing I can walk out of a movie having forgotten about completely, and then it hits me the way you wake up after someone you love has died and have that early morning moment where you remember they're gone.

No cigarette prayers this morning, just lots of cigarettes, and the loud waves and the sight of a beautiful woman picking up seashells down at the water's edge. I watched her for a long time, thought of the woman I've crushed on these last ten years or so. I've put her off like crazy and she still stays in friendship with me, has no idea that I keep away for the reasons that I do. And this beach woman just kept at the shell choosing, never tired of it. By the time she walked back up the hill her arms were overloaded with treasures.

I'm coming into the language that fits for me. The word *lesbian* sounds weird. Lisa the Therapist said to me, "What are you sure of?" I am sure that I am attracted to women, and that I have been for as long as I can remember. "Then say that," she said. So I am. And I sat with two more friends in the last few days. I said that. Both were loving and open-armed to me in their own ways, a relief.

I can see the rubber band ball of all the pain that I am currently causing and will cause and have to keep telling myself that I don't have the hands to unravel it all and make it right for everybody. I have given myself this job, though, for so many years that it is a constant decision not to run out, and to try to make everybody feel better, not to explain it all away, agree not to go back and just say sorry, not make all this trouble.

"Where are you in all of that?" Lisa the Therapist keeps asking me when I tell her, well, just about anything I tell her. I'm not much of anywhere. Haven't been for so long. I've sidelined myself, redshirted for life.

It's the out ahead that's got me stumped. I start to imagine myself alone, my husband here with the kids, my husband with the new wife who will surely arrive sooner than I want her to.

TRAJECTORY

I saw a movie about a man stuck on Mars, and a scene where the young astrophysicist envisions the wild possibility of a lost astronaut's rescue. He rips a map off a wall, grabs a ruler and plots the astronaut's landing place, plots the place where the orbiting spacecraft is already in the sky and then flings out a line to the place where the rescue could actually happen, a point in space where nobody is yet, but where everyone is on course to be.

And I try to believe this about the where that I have been and the where that I am. I try to believe that the where that I will be is a rescued spot out ahead, to believe that the trajectory of this chapter is one of hope and not only loss.

But as much of a glass half full sort of person that I've always been for everybody I love, I am the first to see all of the ways that make that hope more like a dream. So now I have to morph my dreams into hopes. I'm tired of not believing it's all possible, so I will. And when I start to wonder if I'm crazy or delusional or daft, I will see that ruler plopped down on the map and the fast drawn line out to reasonable hope.

GAY 101

I wonder: where will I find Gay 101, the sort that I'm craving, the kind that helps me know whose eyes to peer into and whose to look away from. How will I learn to make a woman deeply, deeply happy, and who will I ever learn with, and when will it begin, and how will I hold on from here to there, and when will my love come to me, and how will I be ready, and how will I wait, and what if I don't?

I asked a good friend the other night: "How do you even know if a woman's a lesbian?" She is not a lesbian, but she is the sort of friend who knows answers to questions like that. This question seems necessary, as I have yet to figure it out. She said, "It's in the eyes—they say you can tell in the eyes."

I sat next to the woman with the beautiful feet tonight, she kept me company on a curb outside the wine bar where a few of us met up, friends whose children were all small and difficult during the same time, and I smoked some cigarettes and we talked. She looks at me so long when I see her, holds her eyes on mine, and one day I'll tell her why I am always the first to look away.

TELLING FRIENDS

I told a really old friend, the one who I'd sat with at linoleum-topped tables in Sunday School when we were two and three, and then for lots of years after. We spent hours at the swings in the church parking lot waiting for our parents to stop talking and take us home to eat whatever was waiting for us in crockpots on our kitchen counters. I spent those after-lunch afternoons on the couch watching old Abbott and Costello movies while my parents retreated to their bedroom. Those daytimes were stuffy and quiet and a countdown to when we would rally and re-dress for night church.

My friend was going home to the same—and also to hitting and exclusion and belittling, the reality of his father's righteous and quiet commitment to whatever demon he spent Sundays likely trying to tell himself he'd already slain. I didn't know this when my friend and I would meet back up at night every Sunday and wander hallways, small groups of us ditching and being ditched by the rest. I didn't know this when we sat together watching cartoon reels forwards and backwards after we'd sat in as much nighttime church pew silence as the grownups thought necessary for proper Christian training. I didn't know this when I spent the night at his house on the bottom of his trundle bed when my parents left town. But I know it now, and the sight of his little unprotected seven year old face pops out at me whenever I see him.

It was evening, drinks poured in front of us, when I sat on his couch across from him and his kind wife and laid it all out. They nodded a lot and looked at me caringly and then she said, "We're not afraid of gay people." And that was a nice thing to hear at the right time to hear it. And then he burst out with the ugliest cry I've seen since I can remember. He was overtaken by it. Not that I'm gay. Not that my family is undeniably punched in the gut and might not get up, but because I told him I had wanted to die. "We can be disappointed but not devastated," he said. He can alliterate even in the worst of times. And their love for me stayed with me when I left, and even longer when they texted me as I drove home, "We love the shit out of you."

And I am glad I sat and drank with them the night I did because the conversation a few days later with my friend of 25 years didn't go as well. She kept saying "collateral damage" to me.

"It's not like you're a teenager. There will be so much collateral damage." And she kept talking and all I kept thinking was *stop saying collateral damage.* "What would it be like to be true to your husband and kids?"

And I said back very slowly and with a squinched look on my face full of the knowledge I wouldn't be understood: "I think that's what I'm doing."

"I still think you should stay and work out the struggle in your marriage, work out your attraction to women. There's so much there with the Lord that you will miss if you don't."

And I didn't think until later to say to her, "My husband doesn't want to do that, and neither do I." I just sat there and nodded, sort of stunned by the fact that there wasn't something I was going to say to connect to her.

She cried when she left, and I know she was crying for my children and also for me, but not because of my pain, because of my choices. And I suspect that she was crying for what could be her forthcoming removal from my life. After sharing children and laughs and vacations and difficult parents and quirky husbands and gallons of wine and honesty together. And I know that was hard for her to drive away from.

"How does it make you feel?" another friend asked me on the way home when I called. And I couldn't muster more than "disappointed," but today I add these words to the list: *undermined, misunderstood, condescended to, judged, seen past, skipped over, patronized.*

When I said "I'm nervous about losing our friendship," she'd just nodded.

WHAT WE SAID #3

We are really good together now. Unangry, unresentful, ungrouchy, un-short with each other. We listen, we smile, we hug and mean it, we make room for each other in the way we're parenting all three kids, we even look at each other with real love. So much love as we come up on parting.

We sat with coffee this morning and talked in alarmingly peaceful honesty, a kind I wouldn't have thought possible a year ago. The defensiveness is gone. And the expectation and the disappointment too, seems like just love and sadness are left, and an impressive amount of realism and resolve on his part. His friends don't understand. His friends are telling him this is my fault. He's telling them it's not.

I don't cry unless I'm with him, and I cry most times I am. We rode our bikes to the movies tonight and I cried most of the ride home. The sight of him in his helmet, pedaling that bike like he always does, and sharing popcorn during the spy movie, and his flat-out regular life kindness to me in the midst of this wretched upheaval in some moments just proves too much, and I cry in a way I never really do or have before, a steady release of tears that comes and just starts to gush and doesn't stop. He made me stop riding so I wouldn't crash, and told me again that it's different than other divorces. "This is who you are," he said. And it struck me then that he is the person loving me best in all of this. I feel more understood by him than any other. And that is at the very least unexpected, and at most the high mark of proof that he's a good man, a man I'm glad I've loved all the years that I have.

CIGARETTE PRAYERS #4

My incoming cigarette prayer today as I sat and watched choppy waves was *Stay*. And this was a sweet word for me to receive, because it's been my soul's primary directive since I prayed at fifteen one of my best prayers ever: "Well, I'm not doing a very good job with my life, so I guess you can try."

It was not many weeks later that I came across the three strangely-placed words at the end of 1 John 2: *Remain in me*. And I heard them like a stout whisper in my ear, like a kind command, a clear method for managing what was coming—all my straying—and the only way to make it through: to remain. So I have. And I got to hear it again this morning. And I said back out loud: *I'll stay forever*. And I meant it. Because like Lucy says of the water in Narnia, "There is no other stream." And because this keeps being the one that quenches my thirst, even now, especially now, as I step away from the version of faith I've known and some of my partners in it, and out toward greater love and honesty with the people who are sticking around.

I breathe in and out more easily than I have before, except for when I don't. And this is a decided improvement in the way my anxiety's shuttled me along over the years.

HAND WRINGING

Jesus, I have so many friends.

I lined them up this morning in my mind—the small set of people who I know are feeling things about me, the ones I would be otherwise spending my day trying to figure out how to soothe or apologize to or give to so that I don't have to feel the weight of the emotions they've got about me, the ones that might mean I've fucked up in some way.

I lined them all up and looked at them. And I saw the thought bubbles of what I figured they'd say to me right now pop up over their heads. None of it was great. Then I told them to go away—the thoughts, I mean, the coming poison of that responsibility I'm so ready to take. Then the friends were all left standing, no sentences hovering over their heads. Some of them took a step toward me, and some stayed put, and one took a big step back.

When I rubbed lotion into my hands this morning, I thought of the women I've seen doing this—using one hand to smooth the lotion around the other, and I realized that maybe lotion gave them the chance to wring their hands. To stand in the middle of their bedroom right in front of the person they were most worried about and act out their worry in a long ritual of beauty. And I wrung mine for a while with lotion—with nobody even around.

I drove home today after three hours with my friend who asks the best questions, and it came to me that I have landed in the middle of a theological, or maybe doctrinal, swirl of Christian disagreement. She was impassioned out of love for me, fearful of my bad decisions, unsure of my insight about the consequences of my actions. I listened and looked at her squarely and openly because she's earned my deep trust. After a couple of hours of listening, I heard something that stopped me, so I doubled back to it with her.

"You said that you feel like this doesn't seem like a smart time for me to make decisions"—two months out from a weeping, suicidal chapter of impulsivity, chock full of high emotion and reckless abandonment to my desires.

"But I understand that I am acknowledging an awareness, not making a decision," I said. This seems the lynchpin of my conversations, I realize: *Am I talking with someone who sees me as a decision-maker or an awareness-finder?*

I sat with this on the drive home, and on the balcony with my bedtime cigarettes, and all the next morning. As I listened to my incoming prayers that night, I got a clear and immediate: *They are wrong.* So I'm teasing out why that could be true, and why I'm finding peace in the middle of all this sadness and upheaval.

I believe it's this: my husband and I haven't failed their idea that same-sex attraction should be overcome inside a marriage; it is their idea that has failed us.

And the reason lives inside the hyphenated phrase they use to describe where I've landed: same-sex attraction. It could be replaced easily with 'alcholism' or 'gambling habit' or 'porn addiction,' any state of mis-managed behavior. It doesn't carry anything like the soul-stamping word gay or queer. To use those words would be to acknowledge that diversion and restriction just don't cut it.

The real truth is that their solution to where we find ourselves just hasn't worked. And for some reason the conversation seems only to include the last two months of my life, of our life together. Both of my closest friends acknowledged that they have been aware of my longtime attraction to women. I've chewed on this. They knew. And I knew. But we never talked about it—I mean we did in small dashes of conversation I initiated any time I found myself inside a magnetizing friendship and was working to divert myself.

I have tried diversion. I have tried denial and reframe. I have tried moving away from encounters not only with women I'm attracted to, but even the music and television shows and movies and groups and churches that acknowledge that a gay person lives in the world. And none of that has worked. I've done it for my 17 years of marriage. And for many years before that. It hasn't worked.

If their take on living with same-sex attraction was feasible for anyone, it would have been for me—because I am wired for responsibility and fitting in and avoidance and a fanatical desire to please and be included. And too I had all the resources anyone would ever need to succeed, even a husband who could hear me hint at small bits of those attractions in the tender, fearful patches of honesty we found over the years. Even friends who I welcomed to speak regularly and directly into my life.

But here is the bald truth: The system doesn't work—and it is a system, as I see it. It's not a belief. It carries the same weight of loyalty, but it has no basis in love, only fear of the loss of righteousness, which is not belief even if it looks like it is. It's an idea built from shreds of language scattershot throughout thousands of words of clearly writ beliefs. The actual beliefs are clear ones, things like:

- Love your neighbor.
- Don't judge.
- Believe that Jesus is who he says he is.
- When you try to guess who is following Jesus, you'll likely guess wrong. So don't.
- Be ready to sit next to people you don't feel ready to sit next to.
- Be ready to give up your coat to somebody you don't want to give it to.
- Love the people others feel sure deserve it the least.
- Don't overestimate righteousness.
- Don't underestimate love.

And I want to say this to them, my friends who are choosing their ideology over their friendship with me:

You all are the proof that your own ideology is broken: If there were any friends who could have provided the compassion and courage to enact it lovingly, it would have been you. You have more capacity for those things than anybody else I know.

But you have failed me. You were content for me to suffer in silence. You encouraged my averting myself from temptation. And you're mad now that I've failed after 17 years of working really hard at it.

It was working because I was bearing the weight of it alone.

And I just can't bear the weight anymore.

And then these other words also, the ones that kept coming to me as I imagined myself sitting with them all—both my friends and their husbands who've been like brothers to me: *Goodbye. I will miss you all terribly.*

TOO MANY FUCKING HEARTFELT EMAILS

I've got an email waiting from my friend who asks the best questions, written to me, well to both of us—actually, probably truly written to our marriage, that third thing. I've left it unopened, mostly. I read the first two paragraphs, the parts where she tells us how much she loves us, but then I stopped. Decided to give myself a break from processing and responding and trying to make others see what I see. Too many intensely-worded emails to name—okay, two. My head is filled with them, and I'm trying to breathe my way through them.

Today I sat with my compassionate friend who is bible smart and told her my whole story. She listened to the whole thing, listened so long she was late to pick up her kids from daycare. She has actively studied the homosexuality issue in the bible, and she told me that people always want her to take a stance, and that she never can, never does, hasn't yet—too much gray, she said. And I told her that I've landed—just by living—into the middle of a doctrinal disagreement, and that I'm living my way out of it. And she said she'd do lots of todays with me, with our family, and that was a real kindness and comfort.

I let myself listen to Barry Manilow this morning. He's such an embarrassing singer to love. But every time he opens his mouth he says something that my 12-year old heart felt deeply. In 1981, I poured out "I Can't Smile Without You" from my heart to the dining room carpet, face down and sprawled out next to the stereo, in love misery over my assistant basketball coach, the one I left when we moved to Oklahoma suddenly in the middle of eighth grade. And this morning "I Made It Through the Rain" was the song for my 48 year old heart, and I sat with it like a prayer outgoing and incoming and let myself feel it all.

LISA THE THERAPIST #3

Lisa the Therapist says that the black ooze I see inside myself, the stuff keeping me sad and anxious, is not me. And it's not in charge of me. I can ladle it out, she says. And I asked for help with that in my cigarette prayers this morning. I have called it "neediness," a false name I've used for wanting connection with someone. I need help for it to go away so that I can go forward and really live. And really love. Really be inside of a love.

I have believed that the black ooze was an infinite pool, but I see now that really it's a deep pool and that I regenerate it with my hiding. So now that I'm not hiding anymore, I can get to it a whole bucketful at a time. Ladling would take too long, like scooping up a swimming pool with my hands.

WHY LESBIANS ARE PUDGY

I get why lesbians are pudgy. It's because when you're coming out everybody is all, "Are you sure?" and then you just want to go eat a bowl of noodles and drink gin.

Then, I imagine, when they stop, you're so relieved that they've stopped that you say, "Let's celebrate!" and then to celebrate you go eat a big bowl of noodles and drink gin.

And then once it's all sunken in to the world around you, and you meet someone and you ask them out, you say: "Hey—wanna go get a bowl of noodles and drink some gin?"

And then later, when your love has happened enough for the nervous outings to subside, and you want to be home with your love, you say: "Wanna just stay home and watch a movie and eat a bowl of noodles and drink some gin?" This is the true story of lesbian weight gain. I'm sure of it.

CIGARETTE PRAYERS #5

This morning I am worried both that I am gay and also not gay enough. Not gay enough for everybody to believe I'm gay. Maybe the category "same-sex attracted" is a subset of gay, a waiting place of the possibly-gay, the purgatory of gayness. Or what if gayness isn't real, or that if it is, I'm not? So I sat down in my chair in the middle of the ice plant and would've buckled myself if I could've and asked: *Dear God, Am I really gay?*

What would my incoming prayer be? Would it be: "It's true. You're only 27% gay."

But it wasn't. It was this: *You're gay, and I love you.* Nobody was more surprised than I was that God is nodding at me as I keep walking forward each day. I still forget for handfuls of minutes and then sort of jump a little inside when I remember: "Oh yeah. I'm gay." And then I nod too. Because it feels true today, and all the days I'm looking at behind me. And I keep trying to wrap my head around the words "design over desire" that popped out of my friend's mouth when we met, the one who'd kept saying "collateral damage,"during the time when she looked mad and worried and before she'd started to cry. I've even let myself get downright sad these last couple of days really considering it. Design over desire. It means they think I wasn't designed to love a woman. And my desire to be loved by a woman is trumped by the reality of being designed to love a man.

I do love a man. I love my husband. I love him deeply. And I've been loving him all of our years of marriage, and I intend to love him until we both die. But we haven't found that landing spot where bodies meet up to share souls. We've tried to. And if I were to be able to find it with anybody, it would be him.

SHAME

I whined to Lisa the Therapist yesterday, showed up like a discouraged punk 16-year-old and told her I just don't think I can do this. It's too hard. She nodded a lot and started trying to help me see my strengths. All I could think of was *Why are you trying to compliment me right now? I just told you I am too weak to do this hard thing.*

I was telling her about sitting with the emails I've gotten from my closest friends, the emails that tell me I'm doing it wrong, that I'm going to devastate my children, that I need to be true to my husband, that I'm still crazy and I'm making unhealthy decisions. She wouldn't let go of the strengths conversation. And it wasn't until some time after I drove away that I got it. *Oh. Right. She sees that I can do it and I don't see it. Got it.*

So I sat at the ice plant and let myself list my strengths. It was a longer list than I expected. And I meant everything I wrote down. I could see everything in me, didn't have to drum up any of it, and they were primarily descriptors of my true self with a few valuable skills thrown in the mix. The weaknesses were real, but a shorter list, and mostly about finances, and that I need to do something about it. And also that I am prone to forgetting who I am. And that I default to humor when I'm nervous.

This morning as I woke up my brain and soul had been colluding together to show me a nice thing about my insides: I'm not needy. This was a shock, because I've told myself that I'm too needy for love and connection for as long as I can remember. *You're not needy: But you are full of desire, powerful desire.* And it makes sense to me today that my draw to women in friendships would be stronger than many of theirs to me, that I've so often been left wanting.

As I rode home on my bike from the ice plant, I could see an oil derrick of black ooze exploding out of me—tar-black shame and the thick, dark brown muck of old lies, the dark weight I've carried all of these years.

I rode home listening to the song that arrived as an incoming prayer, a claiming of me from the God I'm just now really getting to know: "You Belong to Me," and it played on even though I felt ready to hear something different, the way I keep waiting to hear something different in all my incoming prayers, something less intimate, something about what I'm supposed to do to earn all of this upfront love, something about paying off all of this love credit.

But nothing different ever comes.

THE BIRD

Yesterday a bird flew into the garage. My back was to it, but my husband saw it and jumped, which made me jump three times as far and also let out a really unattractive lady scream. He went to look, and there it was: the little bird had smacked the back garage window and landed dead into the hand-painted pottery coffee mug I'd made him for our first anniversary: the one with all our private messages painted beneath a grayish veneer of sort of secrecy: *Husband and wife rhymes with life; 4-4-98*, our anniversary; and a really dear and true and shy thing we said to each other so often then, painted on the bottom so that it appeared when you'd finished all the coffee.

And there was the dead bird, the bird that could've landed anywhere, at its life's end in that cup. *Fucking metaphors everywhere*, I thought and shook my head. *Why do they have to be everywhere?*

And then hours later he came in and said the bird had made it. He'd walked into the garage and seen its little head popped up above the cup. "Must've just been stunned," he said. He'd opened a window so it could be free. And I said, "Oh good," and nodded my head and let that image stay with me, breathed through the end of the metaphor.

WEIRD NORMAL

It would be one thing to spend the bulk of most days questioning and being questioned about why and how I'm a gay, but there are all of these other conversations now at home too: How will we have enough money for two places to live? How will we share a house with the kids but still have the amount of privacy we need to do our personal lives too? And also there's all the groceries the kids keep eating. And phone bills, monstrous phone bills. And the seven year old with her stories, and the dog who needs a flea bath, badly. There's the driving to water polo games and to cooking lessons. So far coming out is a combination of surreal and regular, an odd combination that wants me to pick between the two constantly. But I won't. I'm living the weirdest normal life I've ever lived.

I sit now at the ice plant in the morning most days, ready to think and hear, but I find myself just sitting in the quiet, sitting with me. My feet get up from that spot at some point to go do the life I'm thinking about. Today there's a job to apply for and lunch to have with people who have no clue what's going on around here and who won't know when we're finished eating either. There's an email to return to another dear fierce friend who doesn't like what my heart wants. She says to turn back. I have yet to know what to type in response to her that will balance love and honesty. All I can see is her disappointed, ruined face when she reads it.

My son ran after me down the hall yesterday, ready finally to confront me with what he's been suspecting—based upon my wretched smoke stink—that I am smoking cigarettes. My husband was in front of me walking and laughing at me, his back to us both and I heard him say, "Buusstteedddd." I pushed him on the shoulder and told him to hurry up so I could hide in the bathroom. It was a no go. My boy caught up to me.

There I was standing across from my son, six foot one and still with such a young face.

"Mom, I want to know if you are smoking cigarettes."

And then I opened my mouth and practiced the conversation I know I'll be having with him sooner than I want to, sooner than he'll want.

I told him, "Remember the time I told you last year that there would likely be a day in your life out ahead when you were really annoyed and probably disappointed in me and wanted nothing to do with me? Well, that might be today."

He didn't remember my ever having said it, so I said it all again. I told him what I'd said before: that no matter how angry or broken away from me he would ever feel, no matter how far off he moves from me, I will stay. That I will be here when he comes back around. And I told him that he would come back around. He nodded. And then he said, "Ok." And we talked about how I'm doing something I'm not proud of, but that I've hit kind of a stressful time and that the cigarettes calm me down and that I don't want him to smoke them even though I am. And he said that seeing me smoke them wouldn't make him want to. Which was a lie of course, but I nodded. Then he stepped forward to hug me, held on to me for telling the truth, I think. And I knew I had just practiced saying what I'd say soon. And I know we'll go forward like this—even if his hug takes much longer next time to meet.

SLOPPY BOOBS

Last night my daughter told me I have sloppy boobs. "Thanks," I said. "This is just what happens to boobs after 40, honey."

"I don't want sloppy boobs," she said. Then I told her not to worry, she'd have perfectly lovely, perky boobs for a long time, and then after she turned forty they'd start to get sloppy.

And I thought then about how my coming love only gets to have my sloppy boobs, and not those small, perfectly round ones I had for so many years with no appreciation whatsoever at the time for their loveliness. These two seem to have broken up with each other, each one trailing off away from the other. I imagine they'll have to do.

EVERYTHING

One of the wisest things my mother ever said to me was something an old man from Arkansas told her: *You can have anything you want; you just can't have everything you want.*

I'm sitting with this again, as I have so many times before. This everything now is living at home with my husband and the kids plus hoping to start my new life too. I've wanted to believe I could do both of these things at the same time. I'm wondering about that now, as my husband moves in and out of real pained grumpiness, a legit state for a man whose wife of seventeen years has just confessed to loving women.

I found myself leaning toward him to try to shake it away from us both this morning. I'd dumped coffee all over his bacon, reached up while he was cooking, grabbed my coffee cup out of the microwave and then proceeded to spill the damn thing all over the stove, and his bacon. These are the moments when his patience is clearly thin, when he's caught off guard, and must be thinking what I am: *we're clearly not meant to be roommates.* But then I look at my kids, their three funny faces, and I know I can't move even a sleeping bag and a pillow out of this place for myself. I really don't feel that I can. And this seems particularly hard since I am aching to, aching to sit at a table that's mine with a woman who's mine, drinking coffee in the morning quiet.

You can have anything you want; you just can't have everything you want. I have no idea right now what my anything will turn out to be. I am crystal clear about my everything, though.

GAY 201

Since I only know one lesbian, and she lives out of town, and since I am essentially a church girl, there seemed no other way to learn about lesbian sex than to google it, which is both dangerous and also how I found myself at about.com for lesbians.

I seriously hope all of what they said is true—all the stuff about lovemaking and how to know if a girl likes you (that one sent me to teenager.about.com), and how to be a good lover and what to do for your first time having sex with a woman, and also a lot about lesbians and dildos that I sort of skimmed but didn't stay on after they said something about strapping it on.

I am leaning toward a life I don't really know a thing about. And I want to know. I'm ready to know, but I'm still on hold, living in a sort of family-filled limbo. I'm hearing Kate Bush sing "Don't Give Up" as my incoming prayer at the iceplant and also Stevie Wonder's "Overjoyed" playing on my soul radio. So many thoughts of kissing. And of laying on our sides in bed and looking at each other and saying all the things there are to say.

CIGARETTE PRAYERS #6

I've been nervous to write down my incoming prayer. I'm sure I heard it wrong, doubled back like I did when I heard *Blessed are you*. I sat and said aloud *I'm sad I'm sad I'm sad*. And then it came and, with it, immediate relief:

She already loves you.

I said, *Are you sure?*

And then incoming, *Why do you doubt me when I give you good news?*

This has been the first time I've really stopped and doubted the God presence of the voice that comes when I listen. Any incoming kindness makes me wince a little and wonder, but this one most of all: *She already loves you.*

Maybe I just don't know who she is. I know I still have to stay on hold. There is too much undone here at home to move forward toward love, but it's hard to hold on. I know that I'm not supposed to make anything happen for love. It's going to come to me. And this makes me nuts too.

Apparently I'll finish a quilt before all this waiting is done. I'm already smoking a pipe in a rocking chair, guess finishing quilts is an easy enough thing to admit to. At least it's not a corn cob pipe. But that shit's a total possibility.

DOROTHY

I am thinking today of Dorothy, my Godmother, sitting at her counter doing a crossword every time I stayed overnight there and woke up and walked out into the kitchen. She'd already been awake for hours, was essentially waiting while I slept, I think now. Waiting to be with me, waiting to look at me and play cards together. Waiting to see my face so she could let herself flip through the memories of my young baby face, the one she took care of and had the chance to hold on to and love every day. She died when I was still too young to get that the fact her little living room cabinet held only baby pictures of me meant something significant. She died before I was old enough to let myself call her Grandma.

Because she wasn't, technically. She wasn't the parent of my parent. She was actually the cousin of my grandfather. She was called Godmother. Most of all she was the presence of an old woman always awash in love for me, never forgetting me, with a ready ear and soft eyes and gifts on every holiday. I remember thinking about calling her Grandma and telling myself I couldn't. I was in my thirties when she died. I flew to Kansas with one of my babies when I'd heard she was failing, and went to her bedside and whispered into her ear that she'd loved me well. "None of it was wasted. It all got in," I'd said. She'd been unresponsive for the days beforehand but she shuddered when I told her. And then within days she died.

Still I didn't call her Grandma to anybody at the church basement potluck or to the pastor who had mentioned me in the homily even though I wasn't listed as kin left behind. I think I was saying then *she was like a grandma to me* or some such shitty nonsense that didn't hit the mark, didn't tell anybody that she'd taught me to play double solitaire and played with me for hundreds of hours, that she let me wear her slinky pajamas, that she looked at me with never-ending sparkle, that she left her china to me when she died, that my baby pictures were still hanging on her wall when she died.

Why do we have to call things what they're supposed to be instead of what they are?

WHAT WE SAID #4

I am aching for comfort today and losing patience in a whiney sort of way—not in that angry, take-charge sort of way that pushes you to do something useful like cleaning out closets of old wrapping paper or figuring out how to do your own toes decently well. Today I'm the kind of impatient that wants me to crawl back in bed and binge watch *The Good Wife*, or maybe start drinking before lunch.

My husband told me this weekend that he "didn't know why we were still talking about this"—the "this" was our marriage. He feels caged without the money to leave and not put the kids and me in a lurch. He's ready to go, he says, and also says he doesn't want to. And that's about the sum of most conversations between us these days: we each say at least two things that are impossible to be true at the same time.

I asked God at the iceplant today *What are my lies?* I can see the barely- spittling well of my old shame, but the lies are still gushing when I look inside. And I'm wondering what they are: the way I've said I can live near him and have no future relationship in my new house? That's surely not true, since all I want for the next chapter of my life is to snuggle on the couch with someone. I don't actually mean it when I tell myself I'll limit myself to snogging in cars. I want to mean it, but I don't really. And I'm lying to myself about how expensive all of this is going to be, what it will take to own a house or even a part of one on my own.

I might be lying about how some of my friends are walking alongside me in this. I've been saying that many of them are great, so accepting, so loving. But I notice too that I'm mostly alone these days. Not too many reach outs, I guess if I'm honest, from the people who I know love me. I imagine they don't know what to say or do. I don't either really. I could use a friend who this doesn't make so sad. And I could use more courage to be with the people who it does sadden.

I might be lying that this divorce will be different from any other. I've been telling myself it's a *marriage transition*. I'm a brilliant re-framer. But talking with my husband this weekend and hearing the tone of his desire to just get away sort of smacks that reframe in the face.

Regular life feels a whole lot like sitting in an airplane that's waiting to take off, an airplane that's waiting on a crowded holiday weekend—the one with the empty fuel tank, the one where the pilot keeps saying you'll take off any time now, the one you sit in scrunched and uncomfortable surrounded by stuffy air trying not to get up and ask to be released from. The one with all of the promise and none of the roll of the wheels.

STILL HERE

For about 60 glorious seconds I thought I had discovered a theologically-sound argument for smoking tobacco: if God made tobacco why would it be bad to smoke? What could be its other purpose? This came over me and I nodded my head and said *yes yes that's it*. And then I thought if God created tobacco, why would it be bad to smoke it?

But then I remembered that maybe the plants were created to produce oxygen. And also it came to me that this is how all 17 years olds think. And I'm 48. I would prefer to blame this temporarily lovely but flawed thinking on the fact that I had just pulled in my first glorious drag of the morning and not on the sporadic immaturity of my authentic soul.

The rush of nicotine brings temporary relief after a week or so of visiting real estate with my husband that we can't afford, of living alongside a very angry spouse who is too kind to yell and so just sort of jabs, of trying to help my son pass his first semester of high school, of job hunting, of trying to force myself to make hot food for the people in my house, of sitting on the phone with a sweet thirty-something who I've mentored since she was 20 and soothing her tears for her loss and surprise about my family, of hearing one of my best friends finally tell me sincerely that she doesn't know if she will be able to walk forward with me in my future life choices, of knowing she is hurting in the midst of her fear that she might lose me and I might lose her, and of watching the checking account hover right above zero with another 10 days in the month.

Every day brings another hard thing to hold.

But I'm still here. And I probably am because of texting so often with my friend Dawn who will say "You are so brave" to me no matter what I tell her, and "They are assholes" whenever I update her on a hard thing I don't want to be angry about.

And probably too because of sitting with a good buddy and telling her who I would kiss if I could, of smoking my pipe on the porch, of walking the sand with the wisest of my friends while she listened to me replay my pain, and of sitting around a table with my mom friends and talking about our stinky sons and about our memories of when their stinkiness was really cute, of playing a handful of games of mancala with my seven year old, of laughing with my middle guy, the one with the old soul, lots and lots of times, of binge watching *The Good Wife* alone and under the covers, of knowing I have no money and making a plan to do something about that, of smoking while I drive and hearing Lisa the Therapist say with her kind, stare-down eyes: *you've been miserable for a really long time, Ginger.* And feeling seen in the midst of the clouds, feeling my own head nod. And of remembering that she's right.

I bounced another check today. So, yeah, *Fuck you, Capitalism* because why can't I just trade beaver hides like all those other people did so that when the lady who sews my leather underpants for me comes calling for her hide, I can just say, *Hold on* and take my beaver gun and go out into the woods with it while she waits in my weird hay shack drinking garden leaf tea and smoking her pipe happily near the fire? This is my question.

It is hard to find anybody to laugh with these days. I mean, of course it is. And also, shit I need to laugh sometimes. The people I usually laugh with are all sitting by the metaphoric side of the road with blankets over them, in shock and sad and sort of fuzzed out. And there is nothing funny about what is happening with me and to me and with and to these dear ones I live with, but if I don't laugh a little, then my heart just starts shifting down into such low gears that I can't make my way from the bed to the fridge.

I told the woman with the beautiful feet last night that I am gay. And we were drinking wine, so I told her to take a nice big gulp before I let her in on why I started smoking. And then I said "I am gay," and she kept her eyes in unfluttered check, just looked steady back at me, completely committed to stay in the game.

Later when I told her that I'd had to go dark with friends over the years, and then even later when I said that she'd probably noticed I'd gone dark with her, and then even later after that when I said: "Honestly, I didn't move in and out of our friendship because you made me mad, I moved in and out of our friendship because the day I met you all I could think was 'She is so so pretty.'"

We walked out to our cars and made plans to go paddle boarding with our friends this weekend, which I knew we wouldn't do. And that was that. I got to say. She got to hear. And that was all. And it was enough.

This week has had big trenches of darkness in it. And I tripped into them, I won't lie. My feet started refusing to move at some point, and I cried like you do when you're somebody who cries—which I'm not. But then Lisa the Therapist reminded me that I'm really smart, and she asked me about the voices in my head, and I told her they were the voices of the friends I've trusted for years and that I trust them more than I trust myself. She nodded, and she asked me what my own voice was saying. I heard it, I heard that voice saying *It's okay to go. You are really who you think you are.*

I peeked at match.com for my county yesterday, and I found this:

- A small passel of women who are super butchy and who scare the shit out of me.
- Another small passel of women who look to own multiple cats.
- A couple of women who surely retired from full time retail at Nordstrom and who I think might be interpreting the age category "38 – 48" in a sort of jazz-like way.
- My son's 7th grade history teacher.

I'm not feeling particularly hopeful for geographical meet-ups. And I'm not feeling particularly hopeful that I don't fit in one of those categories.

CIGARETTE PRAYERS #7

Today's incoming cigarette prayer: *You're Gay, you're not gay. Whatever. I love you.* It was a declaration of irrelevance, not definition, a perfect response to the coming-out statement it seems like I still have to make every day: "I'm gay." The incoming prayer was a sort of, "I love you. Who cares?" A kindness, the acceptance that big things are often really quite small in the face of loving.

It's the response I always hope for when I tell a close friend that it turns out I'm not who I or they had thought I was. Or, really, that I am exactly who I know I've always been. I'm not declaring anything new. I am accepting something quite old.

The waves today are not the baptizing kind. They're the kind that kill you if you face them down. Only surfers tackle these. You can stay alive if you ride the top of them. But get out from underneath or you're a goner.

BEGINNING

I'D GO OUT WITH YOU

I talked to an actual girl tonight.

She and I walked out to the front of a pub for a smoke. We'd had beers with the girls and stole away for a nicotine hit. She showed me her vape pen and I teased her for smoking nectarine oil. The beers made me ready to share, so I laid it out right there on her lap—the last six months for me, the awarenesses and longings and sadness and waiting and all of it. With fewer words than usual, but still the heart of all of it.

"I've wondered that about myself," she said when I told her.

And then words came to my lips that I tilted my head forward in an effort to see if they'd fall out unspoken, but they didn't. So I took a small breath and said "That would be good news."

"Why?" she said.

"So I could ask you out."

There it was. And I didn't have the weight of worry or even care about how she'd respond, so tired from the day of conversations and hearing more from sad friends about how my life was going to give my kids a story that they'd have to bear. And how I was missing a chance for healing.

So when she blurted, "I'd go out with you," it was a full stop.

We smiled and kept talking. I sat near her and listened, sometimes with my arm rested on the bench behind her so that I briefly touched the soft place above her elbow from time to time. And that was all. We hugged goodbye and said we'd get together again soon, talk more. There was the hint of knowing there might be kissing with the talking, but only the hint. And I left smiling that a girl could like me, maybe even already might.

This morning when my husband asked to sit and talk, I was already chewing on whether to tell him that the road was starting to move beneath me, tell him while there wasn't much to tell. He wanted to apologize for his grouchiness, and tell me again that he is sad and angry and doesn't know where to put it all, what with us here together in the house. And then we talked about the timeline again—that moving apart had to wait until I had a job, until we could afford even a little extra place for him to retreat to while we navigate our way through sharing kids in this house.

My heart told me to tell him, that to hold it would be a lie. And because I want to keep owning my own pace and not leave our moving apart to lie mostly on his shoulders.

"I have another attraction," I told him.

His face got stony and he spoke quickly, words I hadn't seen coming, in a tone I never hear from him: "If you want this to get ugly, then go ahead and pursue that. But you can expect me to throw your clothes on the street and call a mediator to get this done right now."

Yes, anger. Yes, sadness. Also an animal fear of humiliation, and his true rights as a husband bubbling hotly at the edges of it all.

I told him I understood. I told him he was right, that we had agreed no dating until we were apart. Then I told him that my heart is burning, and that my ache seems harder to carry now than even before.

A few tears, and a "Could you let me?" And his, "No."

Not until I have a job. Not until we have a clearly laid out plan. Not while we are under the same roof. And writing it here makes the threat and fatherliness of it all glare like a flashlight in the face, but hearing it I stayed calm and let my choices sit next to each other. And I let myself look at them there.

I'm chewing through what I will tell her when I see her next—tomorrow, actually. I think I've landed on a clear declaration of necessary, temporary friendship that I can offer up on a tender enough plate that she'll receive it like a gift. At least I hope she will.

WHAT WE SAID #5

Today is the day I will open up a spreadsheet and crunch the numbers on my next life. There is going to be complicated addition and also some creative financing. I will figure it out. The money will be somewhere, hiding under some equity rock likely. And I told my husband it's time for us to be in separate places. I told him that I don't want to be apart so that I can date. I want to be apart because I'm ready to. And he's been ready for a while, saying over and over again that he needs space to grieve. So it's time.

I'll borrow thousands of dollars before I'll let us stay under the same roof mad and unhappy and jonesing to go. Tens of thousands, probably. And it won't be wasted even a bit.

I said all of this to him with warm eyes, and I told him again that there was nothing he could do differently, that it's not his fault. He said he might need me to say that to him a few more times. And I told him I would.

THE GIRL WHO LIKES ME OR MIGHT

The girl who likes me or might was deliciously elegant even in her sweatpants. We sat on her balcony, and I smoked a stack of cigarettes and lit and relit my pipe 100 times while she sat quietly with her vape pen, with bursts of big smiles and so many really, truly lovely questions and interests. And then I did the thing that I tend to do—I snuck from her some assurances to try to fill the cup of my nervousness.

She gave me some—her eyes and the way they held mine with them just past the moment when anybody else would look away, and another look later with a flash at the end of her smile, and the thoughtful questions about my journey right now, and even a story about making out with a girl one time. I felt nervous but on solid footing enough to sit inside our friendship. And I still see kissing her some day.

But then I asked her an impossible question: "When I ask you out, will you say 'yes'?"

She was gracious, gave me a "it depends on my situation" sort of answer, didn't want to cheat on the boyfriend she is honest enough to say she doesn't spark with but does love after so much time. My face flushed, I think. I need to stop talking about love and start offering up some, more kissing and less promises of kissing to come.

"I'm not smooth," I kept saying as I wove my way through our two-hour mix of comfortable, honest, story-telling conversation and my meager, vulnerable flirtations. I felt like I was pedaling a wobbly bike through beautiful fields. She hugged me before I left, held on a little. There are no guarantees available to me, no promises and no assurances that I will not have love kindly rejected, which will hurt terribly, even if it is with a soft hand.

I left and drove to the ice plant and talked myself back to a steady place. I'd been ready to let her know I couldn't ask her out yet, and she'd been ready to tell me she couldn't go if I did. Those two pebbles gummed up the otherwise smooth works of a visit overlooking the Pacific Ocean that was the best part of my day.

I can see myself sitting there at the iceplant with my last cigarette of the day, talking to myself sweetly about how to do a better job next time, and I want to tap myself on the shoulder and hand myself those two pesky rocks of expectation and point out to the big sea where they need to be flung so that I can sit on more balconies and drink more beers and smoke more pipes with more beautiful women and have the moments be lovely and gift enough.

GOALS #2

I will let myself touch people the way that my hands and heart naturally and unself-consciously want to. I don't want to put my hand immediately down anyone's shirt the way that kid did to me in the backseat of the Nazarene church van when I was 12. I want only for my warm love to be given when it's there waiting to be given. I have been that nervous superhero for so long who realizes she has the power to send electricity from her hands, staring down at them there in a dark back alley at the moment she realizes she has the power to do it, nervous and practicing shooting out the wild energy at brick walls where no one can see her try. But nobody will be burned by what I have to send. And it's time to take my hands out of their worn, scorched pockets and let them be in the air and the light where they're meant to live.

I will narrate my heart less and use it more. I am a trained sportscaster of my soul, explaining what it's doing and could have done, used to do before, might do in the future. It's time to push my chair back from the microphone, step out of the box and walk down the steep stairs, shed my jacket, and walk onto the field.

I will stop planning for the moment I will next feel pain. It's time to discipline my nervous, tender heart to believe that the person near me wants to be near me and stop checking the exits for an escape plan all of the time. I seem to live like some traumatized victim of a house bombing when I'm near the soul of warm, beautiful person. Like I might make the spark that explodes them, and I'll be sitting unexpectedly in their blast zone, stupid and hurt and to blame for the wreckage.

STILL NOT CALLING IT *DIVORCE*

I sat in Lisa the Therapist's office last week in tears, and she sent me out at the end of our time to find the friends who could love and support and nurture me. So I reached out to my buddy Dawn who I have mind melded with over the years and also to a couple of other friends. I hadn't thought much about their stories. Three of the four of them leaned toward me and offered kindnesses from their own experiences of divorce. Seems like it must be what I need.

But I have to say that I can barely wrap my mind around the word *divorce* for myself. I'm still using the phrase *marriage transition* to keep my breathing steady, but it looks to be the real thing, the real divorce thing I mean. It's just not sinking in, I guess. The part that is landing is my readiness to be in my own space and let him be in his. And the part about being ready for next love.

I have been really surprised by the way that the universal message from those I talk with is that we all lose friends in this—one friend of mine who lost her husband to sickness a few years back said it happened to her too. Somehow I saw this from the outside when my parents split, and I guessed it about my own coming out, but the divorce piece hadn't shown up for me. I didn't think of the people we might lose if we were no longer together. That's probably because I still haven't even begun to imagine that we will no longer be together.

I have no in-play emotions about this that even begin to match the size of it, just a compelling sense that my feet are walking the road they're meant for. If I were living more than a single day at a time right now, I would say that's not enough. But on this day it is, has to be.

My buddy Dawn wrote to me:

> The thing is, the people in your life who love you—for reals love you—will always love you. They might have to go away for a while, or yell, or get weird, or make it about them (note: these will be the hardest and most puzzling and will be masked as something you won't understand until later), but they'll

keep loving you, and they'll come back if they go, and most will be there through it all (others sporadically or in and out), and when the dust settles and the smoke clears, you'll have your people right there beside you. The ones who go for good aren't your people, even if you thought they were. And chances are it's because they have stuff they haven't faced or dealt with, or they're choosing to live unhappy, dishonest lives. Whatever their pathology, it isn't you.

I plan on reading her paragraph every day, the way you reread a reminder sticky note on your bathroom mirror, or the lines under your own eyes in that same mirror, or the framed little something that sits on your desk—the one everybody thinks is just a saying, but you hold on to like a lifeline truth.

I'm staying committedly inside of friendship with the girl who likes me or might, but I'm building a list of songs to play for her one day. Joanna Chase, "Let Go Gently Girl" to start, and many more that I know it's nowhere near time to play. This stomach flutter for her pulls me back to my chair on the balcony to sit and look out at the water and just feel.

GOALS #3

I will stop drinking near beautiful women because nervous drinking leads to vomiting. I started my day by hosing down and sweeping off the barf I left on the street last night after a liquor-filled night out. And yeah, I barfed: right out my car door, plopped onto a street where kids walk to school.

I will write love notes. It is time to begin writing the love notes I can't yet send. I haven't let myself even compose them before, much less pick up a pen or sit to type. The words have always sat so heavily and ashamedly at the bottom of my stomach that it felt like a kind of stupid extra pain to think of making them real. But my head and heart are writing them now, and I've got to get them down.

LOVE NOTE

I didn't write the note I sat down to write last night. I thought I would write one to the girl who likes me or might about how her smooth shoulder was just inches from me the other night, exposed there because the wide neckline of her top had fallen just a bit. I know we talked that night, but I don't know what we said, because I was just being near her shoulder. And it took me up completely.

I wrote instead to another girl, one from years ago, my first penciled love for her. It will stay in my journal, all of its words, even the ones that end with "I wish…" But I won't tape this one closed like I did twenty years ago for the first girl I loved. That one is still taped shut somewhere in a bucket of journals. I've never untaped it, but I've never thrown it away either.

I hope today I write one I might actually send. I've had more time to think about the other night, to remember. I can replay the end of the night now, there by my car door. Her offering up an end-of-night hug, and the way I held on and just kept saying "I don't want you to settle." I'm pretty sure I even copped a small side feel down the side of her jacket while we stood there. I was saying, "You deserve to be loved every day," and she was saying "You do too."

Then I said out loud a thing that's been percolating in me for weeks: "It's not the getting for me, it's the giving." There's no way she knew what I meant, and no way she knew how much I meant it, but I've been looking at this ache of mine, staring at it intently enough to see that most of what my soul wants is to give the love I've got. I know there must be no love received like the love of a woman tenderized, but I can't even see that far out ahead into love.

I think about the fast-moving touches of panting urgency and the light lift of that space, but I think more about the moments at the end of the day when all the world's dropped at the doorstep and there is just one soul to remind of what home means, of light touches to the small of her back, standing at the stove, of holding a face and of whispering love truth and of pulling on the tether of her bound heart, of bringing her in near where it's safe.

It is the loving and touching I want to give that's got me flaming sore.

CIGARETTE PRAYERS #8

The waves are big and the sky is gray. Hundreds of little plovers are chasing the skinny tide and then rushing up the beach as it chases them back. Must be something there beneath the newly churned sand they feel they've got to have.

The beak of my little ceramic desk bird broke today. It is one of a pair, both metaphoric—The Bird that Watches and the Bird that Sings, those two conjoined pieces of the soul. I've been trying to understand them for twenty years, ever since the kind therapist of my thirties offered their picture to me as a way to balance my constantly-hovering self. And so I am particularly annoyed at Mother Gravity for the attack.

I live so much as the watching bird. I want to live more as the one that sings, there on the wire with no thought of the ground below, not calculating and planning for winter, not stiff with worry and afraid to step out to just see. I will call the broken-beaked beauty the seer. It is in one piece but marred, waiting to be repaired. The one that is still whole will be the one who's meant to sing.

I noticed a brown wash of sun stain across the left side of my neck yesterday—there because the sun comes at me in the morning from that side when I sit at the ice plant. A mark on me from that place.

It was bitterly cold at the waves today. I wrapped myself in my favorite polyester quilt and shrouded my head like the Virgin to keep from having to leave, and I had some smokes. There were no prayers coming or going today, just the warm peace of sitting near Jesus and being welcomed to stay. As the cold is coming in, I have turned my chair a little more each day to meet the warmth.

THROWING ROCKS

My husband and I sat with close-in friends this weekend, friends whose honesty we've welcomed over many years, friends whose honesty has been coming now in spurts of disbelief and anger. And it was as awful as I'd anticipated it would be. I won't write here all they said. Instead I jotted all those hurting words down on slips of paper and taped them to rocks. I'll be throwing them into the ocean when I am ready, throwing them as far from me as I can, and I know I'll wish I'd been a baseball player or a discus thrower or a javelin champ. I want to have to squint when I see them drop in the water.

They'd said all of those things to me while we sat at an old wood picnic table that overlooked miles of vineyards and soft rolling hills, a table we'd all shared together before, many times. The times before there was wine and cheese. This time the table was bare. One husband started in first. I know he said he was mad at me. I know he said, 'So you think Jesus is telling you to leave your husband and your children,' and I know that my husband finally piped in and said that I wasn't leaving my children—though he never did say out loud that we'd decided all of this together, that our parting was a shared one. I know that the one who said he was mad at me hugged me before we left and told me he wasn't mad at me, but then wrote me a letter shortly after telling me that he was.

I know that the other husband there, my dearest friend's, the one who has been a brother to me since my early twenties when he allowed his wife to fold me into their family, he heard me say I'd wanted to die and he stopped me and looked at me, really saw me, and said "I'm so sorry." And I know that those were the only words that landed like love for me in the hour or two we all sat on that hilltop in the cold wind.

I'd decided to let them speak. I'd decided too that I wouldn't say much. Because I knew that my heart was sure footed, but that I would never match up to their arguments. I'd never meet their model of how I was meant to be living. And even though I was sure, my heart was just too sore to put up any sort of fight. I'd decided to arrive willing and veiled.

I know they didn't ask me any questions—not any questions that were actually questions. They made lots of statements with question marks at the end, but there wasn't anyone there who wanted to know how I was, what I'd gone through, how badly I was still hurting, how pulled I was between loving my family and not wanting to let my soul whither, how much I loved my husband and hated to see him hurting. I had disappointed them, and in a way that it looked as though I couldn't or wouldn't be able to remedy.

They were saying their pieces here at this picnic table, practicing the stories they'd need to tell later, maybe, when people asked them how I was, people who knew we'd all been friends for twenty five years or so. And I know now that they were likely more sad than angry, that their anger was at me for forcing them to reject me, because they weren't allowed to accept the reality of my declaration, not and still hold on to the version of the faith they'd been carrying for a collective 100 years or so. They weren't allowed to say *we see you, and we can love you as you are and help your family forward*. And this made them incredibly mad, I think, because they knew how much they'd miss me. I was their friend, after all, their close friend. They did not want to have to lose me.

Which is why I did not write their words down anywhere but for the rocks I knew I'd throw. They wouldn't want me to remember their words anymore than I'd want to. They were words we'd all be glad to have flung far far away.

Later, I dumped all my rocks on the floor at the feet of Lisa the Therapist. And she leaned forward in her chair and held the little vinyl case I'd brought them in. She held it like you would your hands for the communion wafer, or an injured bird. I read my rocks to her one at a time and dropped them back in to the case held there between her hands. I let the hurt of them sink in just enough so that I wouldn't throw them into the ocean out of anger or disillusionment or with the fear they'd come back to me on some strong current someday. I wanted to throw them to release them, to let them go, not to hit somebody with them.

I told her about every last one, and then zipped that case when I left. "Have fun throwing those," she said when I left. And it hadn't occurred to me to make the moment a celebration or any sort of triumph. So I am considering searching for the perfect circus music to play while I stand at the end of that cliff to flail them into the beyond. But it will be a rough soundtrack to get right.

WHAT WE SAID #6

He saw that time differently, he said this morning, that time with our friends spluttering their shock and pain at us on the hilltop. He left the weekend meetup challenged to stay together. He was humble when he talked to me about it, quick to tell the story of his part in frustrating me over the years. "Maybe I shouldn't have released you so easily," and it sounded like he was talking to himself in a car, his tone like stumping reflection more than a loving plea directed to me—both dear offerings, but different sorts.

He's sad to let our family go. And it is still unimaginable to me. "What would you need for us to make this work?" he asked.

And then I had to say, "If hypothetically I were not drawn to women, then…" and I did have things to tell him. Things that all of my churning sexuality aside I won't go back to life with, the parts of our marriage we kept pointing to but never kicked out the door somehow.

It was a merry-go-round of a conversation and left me a little sick. It is easier for me in the moments when we choose this marriage shift together. I see that I may not get the partnership help after all. I may have to stand alone at the edge of my soul, may have to believe by myself that somehow we will cobble together a family frame sturdy enough for our kids to see real love and know that the ground beneath them is steady.

ONE STORY

I spent my twenties trying to write the one story that was my parents' marriage, the one that captured What Really Happened during all of the loudly non-verbal, church-filled years of my only-child life. They split when I was 18—Dad walked into my room wringing his hands and told me he needed to leave, and that I could come with. That he'd tell my mother very soon. It was two days before my high school graduation. I wanted to go with him, didn't want to stay and watch her trying to love him when he didn't love her back any more.

And we did go. About a week later he packed his things in a truck. I was ready with my room boxed when it came. She found my boxes after he told her he was leaving, and before I told her I was. She called me at my friend's house where we were playing quarters with Coors Light and said "Ginger?" into the phone in a way that made me know she was standing in my empty room surrounded by boxes.

That's most of what I can say about the days of knowing my parents were splitting before my mother did. There were lunches with grandparents at some point and a sort of ceremonial gifting of a pearl necklace that I knew was expensive because of the box it came in. My parents gave it to me, the both of them, with meaningful looks about my coming womanhood, believing somehow that the necklace was the best thing to get me set for the life that was coming my way.

There was also a short overnight to the lake with my friends in there somewhere, not a single one of the scenes of which remain with me. I know that I went only because my friends have told me that we did go. And there was the plan my Dad made to signal me on my return from the lake: the curtains would be open if he'd told her he was going to leave. They'd be shut if he hadn't. Also at some point before we even left for the lake, I walked the aisle in a fancy dress I felt stiff and self-conscious to wear and somebody handed me an embossed piece of paper to say that high school was over.

None of those parts of their divorce story have shifted at all over the years. The parts up for re-translating tell how he couldn't try anymore, that she needed him to try forever, and that I was complicit in the leaving—the double-whammy of her worst day.

But in the thirty years since then, their story has been riding in a sort of rudderless skiff on high waters, pointing in every imaginable direction in an effort to land finally in a place that would let me draw one of those maps that is always in the beginning of a really good adventure story—where the countries are named, and little dotted lines show the protagonist's route from start to finish.

Sometimes their story became that he was selfish and left her on her hands and knees. Other times she was the one, in all of her weeping years of dependence, that drove him to his break. Or they were wasteful with the years, or they were helpless to do anything else, both of them sent out into their own lives with so little means of steering themselves to anywhere else than where they ultimately landed.

At some point I stopped trying to find their story. I decided that there wasn't one, not a single one at least. There were, instead, stacks of stories laid upon one another, all of which could never have possibly happened, and still all of which were true.

I am gut-punched these days by the way our story will take the same route for our children. There are already old friends now who have a version that they're ready to tell: that I was the infidel, broke trust with a man who could otherwise have loved me better than any other I would ever again find. That I was a gambler, setting out for a possible love that might not ever cross my path, might not in fact even exist. And that I followed my heart instead of my God.

From what I can tell, I have roughly a month to keep the story from including the sort of scenes that my parents' story did: of screaming exes at the doors of new girlfriends, of angry and exhausted retreat on one parent's part and ruined, dogged clinging on the part of the other. And of the bumpy storyline that keeps swapping the name of the good guy and the bad guy in every chapter.

THE GIRL WHO LIKES ME OR MIGHT #2

I went to see the girl who likes me or might today so that I could look her in the eye after our night's texting about the possibility of love, and her clear "no" to me, after my night of crying and asking her to reconsider. I went to claim the friendship. She was as real and beautiful and kind and funny and open-hearted and accepting and loving and unafraid as a person worth loving could ever be.

Today I stay in bed, the place where sore people need to be. Today, too, I can see the clear line of my hope trajectory, and I am walking straight atop it again. I have been hanging by strained hands this last week or so, could even see myself sort of swinging from a high line I'd fallen from and had grabbed on the way down. I got my armpits over the thing this morning at her kitchen counter, drinking her almond milk latte and laying out the rules of our friendship: No more jokes about wanting to kiss her. No more pointing to the tension or looping her into false nonverbal hints of possible love. Just friendship and our shared want to have it together as we each face our respective shitstorms.

I don't have to be nervous anymore, and I plan on having to remember not to be. I need the comfort of her soft company, her way of hearing me, and the laughing too badly to slink away embarrassed or unwilling to bend. She's worth the reboot of my heart.

A GOODBYE

One of the angry friends from the picnic table called today as I pulled away from Lisa the Therapist's office, just moments after Lisa said to me: "You don't have to fill all of the spaces." Moments after, I sat with my eyes big and said one short "Fuck" because I knew she was right, and that this is how I have lived inside of friendship all of these years. Until now. If there is a space, a sacrifice, a favor, an extra hour, a mile to drive, I fill it, give it or drive it. I don't give anyone a chance to fill that space for me. This was floating in me when the friend called.

She went almost immediately to apology. She apologized for not coming alongside me the way she wished she had in the months that led up to today. There was a strain in her voice that I know well—the one that comes when her heart is so full of love and hurt that it's in her body like a chest pain would be, and her breathing seems tight and her voice shrinks back.

She offered up her true sorry from all angles, and each from the same aching place in her heart—the one where love and hurt meet. She asked for forgiveness, and I gave it quickly, so relieved as I was to be able to offer something to her in these months of being apart. I have missed her. I told her of my real hurt, of the feeling of lambast and the disappointment.

Then I released her.

She would have gotten off of the phone, I think, but I asked her to wait, softened down my voice so she could hear it best and told her thank you for all of the particular gifts she'd given to me over so many years, and that I would always be grateful for her, that I would keep hearing from God the way that she'd trained me to. And that I understand.

Then we said goodbye.

It was the sort of parting two friends make when one is about to board a ship and the other is staying on the land. I feel grateful for it, some of the rocks inside me thrown off before I've even yet driven to the cliffs to throw the real ones. The reality that she may be truly gone from me doesn't even have a space to fit in my heart today. Today there is only the lifted weight. I know the other will come. And it will be a new weight, though wholly uncomplicated, and therefore both terrible and bearable.

I drove away when we hung up and pushed play on my shuffled group of songs, and there was Justin Bieber, my least likely writer of prayers, singing "Purpose," giving me the one that I sing out as my outgoing for the day, not to a lover or to my children, but to my God.

DRINKING SAND

This is the time of year when the beach drives everyone away—gray and cold and with a wind that makes you want to stay in your car, or in your house. Maybe it doesn't want us to see what a mess it can be, one line of surf toppling over the next, with just a slightly discernible line between where one begins and another ends.

I stand in the ice plant to offer up my outgoing prayer: *Thank you for the comfort.* The wind buffers me, and I hear the incoming: *Get to where it's warm,* so I do.

I sat in my car to finish a cigarette. It is hard to hear prayers this morning over the din of my heart and the voice of Tony Bennett singing "Time After Time." I did get a *You're good* through the windshield, Jesus forever unpanicked and unafraid of the way my heart bobs on love.

I am starved of intimacy, so thirsty. I can see that I am the man who has crossed the desert, the one who sees an oasis just ahead wherever he goes, a picture of just enough hope to make him ignore his blistered feet and his sun-scorched head or the way the thirst is making his brain buzz with rage. And here I am at the edge of the oasis, a pool of real water. I am that man throwing himself at the water, guzzling it until he makes himself sick. Drinking again and vomiting again, over and over while his head says *just sip* and his body dives his face back toward the water.

Somehow the girl who likes me or might stays calm and smiling through this repeated exercise, her feet in place, with very few words and a constant willingness to stay near and not run while I struggle gulping and retching by her side. I see only the water right now, and I want to see her. *I won't steal love. I won't beg for love or steal it anymore.* This morning I reread the promise I made two months ago in its original form:

> *I will not steal love. I will wait to have love offered and I will take it in whatever size it comes. Small kisses, long hugs, short ones. Real looks. Deeper love, all the sex that makes its way to me. I won't steal any. I won't talk anybody into anything or stand at the edges of possibilities, hopeful and wanting.*

I am not pulling this off today. Or yesterday, or for a few weeks now actually. I am standing at the edge of possibility, *hopeful and wanting.*

I am gulping up the water that's not even here yet. I am face deep in a sandy version of the love that I am desperately thirsty for.

She sees my love. Sits on the other end of the declarations of my devotion and my desire and doesn't stop being there. Doesn't go away. Doesn't answer. And doesn't respond. And when I say *I feel foolish* she says *don't feel foolish*, but I do. Because my heart feels like it is entirely hers and she wants only pieces of it and is somehow not put off by the pieces she doesn't want. But I am aching for her, waiting for her to want the whole of me, dying to be the one who loves her completely while the world pushes in and we push it back together. If she'd let me. And I don't know if this makes me a stellar lover or a fool.

Someone is going to receive the full gift of my thirty years of waiting to love. And I want so badly for it to be her. Someone is going to receive the gift of giving her deep, abiding, awake love. Someone is going to take that face in their hands every day and kiss it and tell that ear what it needs to hear, only the things that are true, and all the things that are true. And I want so badly for it to be me. It may not be. And it may be. And I fear I don't get to make that call.

WHAT WE SAID #7

My husband and I sat with the counselors today—his and mine—and talked through what it might look like to sit with our kids and let them know what's going on. I was strangely quiet-hearted, quite calm really. There's such an inevitability around these conversations that somehow settles me more than gives me despair. I did feel sad looking at him. His eyes are still warm—not when they talk about us, but still when he looks at me. And I know he is both saddened and resigned and also really angry.

So far he is offering up the resigned to me, peppered with willingness. We drank a beer afterwards and made a list of what might work so that we could keep in touch enough to actually co-parent and not just hand kids back and forth. I know that I'm experiencing this shift differently than everyone else. I've got a belly full of relief mixed in with the sadness and the disappointment of having given up on something we tried really hard at. Nobody else has that in their mix. It's lonely, actually. Still calm, but lonely.

CIGARETTE PRAYERS #9

It is a sit in the car sort of beach day—so cold with the wind. It chases off the fog, but I didn't bring a big enough jacket to swing being out in it today. Incoming from Jesus here in the car: *I like you more than you like me.* That's nice to hear, especially now.

The girl who likes me or might has me reading about living in the present moment, and I sit and talk with her about it and look at her sweet face and think, "Will you love me someday?" I'm clearly missing the point.

I notice the waves and the smoke of my pipe and my own still heart. I hope I can change from being a person who believes I like everybody more than they like me into somebody who stops wondering. This is, of course, the world's saddest-sounding New Year's resolution ever. But it'll be mine when this year breaks into the next one. I'm going to tell people that it's Health or Yoga or some bullshit, but it's going to be this head flip that I need. What if most people already like me?

I got my second no from her last night—or my third maybe? I went to bed with tears and woke up with a clear head and heart again. She's offered me real true friendship at a time when I could really use it, so I'm taking her up on it. Really this time.

I will put this love in me someplace else, I guess. Or at least pieces of it. So far I am boldly attracted to women who are boldly attracted to men, so I've got some figuring out to do there. And my heart seems entirely un-protectable to me, like a soft, light thing in high winds.

TELLING THEM

We told our teenage boys yesterday. Both of them were loving, wanting to support me. And then from my Older: "Wait—are you gay or bi?" and it came over his face that what I was telling him wasn't about only me, but about his Dad too, about our being together. I said, "I'm gay, honey" and with that he saw that his Dad and I would be parting. All of that knowledge flushed straight into his cheeks and he put his head forward and cried, really cried. We held on to him, his Dad and me, and he held on to us.

Our younger boy acted like a grown up, as he does, kept saying "okaaaaaaay" with a long hold in the middle, a sort of indicator that he was taking it all in and wasn't ready to let us know what he thought about what we were telling him. It will take him more time to feel. He wants to be the one who makes this okay for all of us.

We told them both that we would always stay connected, that we were always both going to be their parents.

Then there were lots of hugs and we pulled off real loving reassurance for them, kept saying to them, "We aren't going anywhere." It is so hard to take in what this means for them, but I know they feel we are with them in it. And now their Dad is going to make us fish tacos. I am having a much-needed after-convo cigarette. I am so glad the first conversation is over. There are plenty more to come, but I'm glad the first one is behind us.

My older son said later, once he'd stopped crying and after he'd heard his Dad tell him it was going to be okay: "I'm proud of Dad for sticking with you." I saw my husband take this in, that he was seen by his son for the good, true man that he is.

My younger son climbed the stairs later to see me before bed and brought the questions that came to him in the shower:

"I know this is personal, but how lesbian are you?"

"Will you have a relationship some time?"

"Did you both agree to this? I'm worried about Dad."

"Will you do the custody thing?" and I said:

"Not sure how you mean it—it's okay to ask though.

"Yes—probably."

"We did—we love each other but didn't see how to stay married with this."

And: "no we won't."

He asked some other things too while he laid next to me in the bed. And then he walked to the stairs and turned to say, "Good job coming out, Mom. It would be bad for you to hold that in there." And I know he meant it. And I know he means many other things that he doesn't know he means yet, but I will be here with him when he knows what those other things are, the things that are for him and not mostly for me.

I woke up this morning before the sun and sat with a cigarette and coffee and watched the light come in. This isn't because it's an "all new day" or anything. It's mostly because I fell asleep after all that telling at about 8:45 last night. My head just wouldn't agree to anymore awakeness.

I'm sitting today in the sort of peace I used to find when I climbed to the top of a trail on my favorite 40 acres in the Sierras at summer camp during high school. It wasn't a big trail, just a small one that led from main camp up to a lookout point. I walked it as often as I could when I was there. I don't remember what the view gave me—it must have been full of trees and far off mountains and big sky. We were at 5,000 feet there, and it was likely July and the sky was a sort of clear blue that only happens at that height. The air smelled like pine trees and dust. I remember the look of the trail. I must have had my head mostly down while I climbed it. I don't remember anybody else ever using the trail, so it felt like mine. It delivered me to a rock perch to look out in some sort of purposefulness at a sky I knew I needed to see alone.

I had my journal with me when I did this. I imagine I wrote in it, though it was the climbing and the sitting that I needed then. And the quiet. And the act of claiming the quiet. And the serious purposefulness of being 17 and trying to know myself well enough to sneak off for quiet from the loud life I chose everywhere else.

This morning's peace is full, the whole cup version of the little vial I felt in me then. Feels like I might have extra to give today as I watch my boys wake into their new real and take their first steps today in sadness and new surety and confusion and willfulness for it all to be okay.

I know that it will be, that it is.

GAY BEAUTY REPORT

The gay beauty report: so far it is *no* to eye shadow, *yes* to mascara. I threw away the dark lipstick I've been wearing for years. Have no idea why I can't now just dress like Johnny Cash the way I always want to anyway. I had already said *no* to shoes with bows. It's a *yes* to pedicures, but the color is still up in the air. And I'm not going to stop bathing or stop getting expensive haircuts. Also *yes* to that under eye concealer that makes you look like a raccoon in pictures but more awake in the bathroom mirror. And *yes* to tweezers with the help of glasses. And *yes* to scent: a custom one made for me by my little sister that I refer to lovingly as "sexy pine trees."

WORKING IT OUT TOGETHER

I can't get over this sleep, this feeling when I lie down. So different, so settled, slow calm. Feels like I've stopped tensing muscles I've had in a grip for years. I think I might be knot-free.

I came out to my best friend from high school over FB Messenger yesterday. Classy move. She was having brunch with her family when she got the message. We laughed our asses off over text, and she couldn't say a thing to her kids.

She said, "I've always known you're gay."

I said, "You could've texted me and let me know 30 years ago."

We're meeting up for booze and more catching up over text tonight. It's time to swap stories and get caught up with each other.

My husband and I have decided to stay together in the house while we figure out the details of our new living set up. We want to let the kids see us working it out together inside our friendship. This is his idea, a really good one. The boys are asking if I'm going to be in a relationship, and I'm saying, "Down the line." I'm saying it to them and to myself.

There is still more telling and more hard-to-read emails and more looking purposefully into the eyes of my children so they see I'm here. More eating dinner in front of the TV with everybody. More bills to pay and more plans to make that there isn't the cash to pay for or make yet. I've got to keep myself open for them all still. I can't use up all of my energy before noon anymore. I've gotta just hold on.

BIBLE STORY

I'm turning back to reading the gospel stories—those books of the bible where Jesus is alive and showing as much as telling us all how to live. I started them again a couple of months ago to scour for anything that might bump me off my road, and so I'm back at them today. I came to the story of the woman who takes her best possession, a really expensive jar of perfume, and dumps it on Jesus' head in a moment of abandon. I wonder what made her think to do it, if she almost talked herself out of it as she walked over to the house where Jesus was eating, if she hesitated, if she'd imagined that moment for a while or if she had some stab to her soul that sent her to grab it and walk up to him in deft reverence and offer it to him as a way of naming who she knew him to be.

She is yelled at immediately by the nearby men in the room for what she could've done with it.

"You could've sold that and fed starving kids in Africa," they say, more or less.

And I've always read this as a sacrificial moment on her part. And also as another bold moment where the men following Jesus don't see him at all and just keep fucking up their chances to be the guys who don't waste their front row seats.

But it looks to me today like she goes to Jesus and pours out her retirement plan upon him actually. She holds on to nothing for her future security, she stops pretending like she knows what's going to come and sees only that she knows who he is, tilts her future on his head as an act of internal declaration: "I have what I need."

And yes, I am her. And no, I have no emotional retirement plan. And yes, there are things I could have done with my own expensive holdings that I'm dumping out for tomorrow. And yes, if I could have met her, I would've said, "Thank you. I'm drafting behind you."

CIGARETTE PRAYERS #10

I drove past the ice plant today and then on further up the coast to have a cigarette in the rain and belted out Lykke Li's "Unrequited Love." I yell-sang it the way she's figured out how to—resolved and real. There is no whining, just telling the truth: "Ohhhhhhhhh my love is unrequiteeeeeeeeed."

Then I doubled back to the beach. The waves are ass-kickers today after a night of storms. It's mucky everywhere. My incoming prayer as I sat in the car and listened for it, my heart already full but still wanting a word: *You. You. You. It's here. Your life is here.*

THE GIRL WHO LIKES ME OR MIGHT #3

I woke up in love again. Incoming: *Hold on.*

It only took holding hands after we'd had some drinks and were sitting with smokes in the dark and saying some of the things out loud we'd only before written down to get through them. We talked about feeling lucky and becoming more ourselves, each of us. I sat near her inside the power of this light peace, all nerves gone, free to give boldly what I had been giving scared and restless. My heart needs to catch up with the news that we are in friendship only and the comfort of morning and night texting check-ins and smoking together and seeing movies. There is still no kissing or going to the places kissing would take us. I don't want to miss the chance for what I've been offered. And my heart has no idea what I mean.

We went to the movies and drank beers last night. We laughed hard and shared popcorn. We sat shoulder to shoulder in cushy movie seats and then at bar stools and talked about life in five years, and the way her heart is standing at a distance from her boyfriend, the difference between honesty and vulnerability. I asked her lots of good questions. I listened and stamped constantly on the internally overfull trash can lid of my pulsing draw to her. I love-trampolined my way through the night.

I'm not sure how this is going to work for me. I know I won't go anywhere. But how do I keep this in? What will it do to me if I turn this new open chapter of my life into a different sort of hiding? Where would I go if I stepped away from her? And why would I? I won't. She is tossing her heart to me, and I am supposed to hold it somehow on the flat of my outstretched arms, like a stack of boxes I might drop.

I came home from the night out to my husband waiting up for me. He looked down at me from his 6'4" and asked for an honest answer to whether I'm in more than friendship with her. I looked at him and told him honestly, "No I am not. I've gotten the clear message that friendship is all that's available to me." And then I told him that I need friends, so many of mine are gone or just stunned, that she has stepped up and I need it.

Then I went to bed with the double whammy of a husband who thinks I'm cheating and a woman who won't let me even if I wanted to. I didn't wake up any clearer about it all, but I do see the crevice I've got myself stuck inside. I've got no clear plan for how I will get out of it. How do gays hold on to beautiful friends without falling in love everywhere they go?

CIGARETTE PRAYERS #11

The incoming message is so strong and steady that I got it today as I opened my car door to grab my orange beach chair for the ice plant: *Hold on.* And then came my immediate *yea, yea* in response.

Then this loving reassurance: *I'm going to give you what you need.* It doesn't take me long to hear these days—and I sit with such relief and say good morning to God, sort of plop into my chair like it's the place I've been waiting all night to land. I feel a palpable welcome. I never sit here alone.

ALCOHONESTY

I have embarked on many a beer-drunken "I love you man" sort of gushing of the soul, slurred and sincere, if maybe ever-so-slightly overstated. Somehow bold and insecure all at once, like a big man playing t-ball.

But tequila honesty: this is a different thing altogether. I rode it like a champ the other night, belted out every fine corner of my love for the girl who likes me or might—even though she says she doesn't—with an intensity of honesty that I had yet to pull off. I emptied the bag of my heart with a couple of shakes at the end to make sure there was nothing left inside.

I'd like to do this sober some time, but for now, I'll settle for the booze boost. I said my piece, said all of my pieces, and woke up with not a single regret, without a bit to retract or explain. And I'm glad for that.

LOVE NOTE #2

How many times can I hear no before I really hear it? What does it take for me to believe? I couldn't count, but I know that whatever it takes has finally happened, and I am determined to remember: *I will not steal love.* I will not wait—embarrassed or ashamed —at the edge of possibility. I will see what I have to give as a gift waiting to be received, not endured. I will be bold and honest, not bold and dishonest. I will listen to what my loves tell me. I will give and then wait. I will save my pearls for the love they're meant for—no pearls to swine.

I will begin to write to her today, the girl who I am meant to love. And someday I'll give her the letter.

Dear Love,

I am having a hard time waiting for you to come. I am spending my heart everywhere, like everyday is the first of the month and I just got paid. I seem to believe that you are hiding somewhere, that if I prod and peel back the layers of the hearts of beautiful women near me, I will find you in there, waiting all along.

So far, my love, you are nowhere to be found. And I am tossing your gifts at the feet of women who don't want to pick them up. I can't seem to convince anyone that they are, in fact, really you.

Please come. Please don't hide any longer. My heart is ready for you, pulled taught at all its edges, and I don't want to waste what's yours on anybody. Anymore.

MY ACTUAL CLOSET

I have cleaned out my closet—the one that holds my clothes. I feel more comfortable in my clothes now. I've found myself quickly and easily giving away the things I don't like, anything that makes me feel like an imposter: short dresses that I thought I would wear in the summertime, a three-quarter-length-sleeve sweater that I bought on sale because I thought I should wear sweaters. And very best: all of my dresses. I've hated to wear them my whole life.

But I've made myself wear them anyway. I wore scratchy dresses to church every Sunday as a kid. I hated them. I remember dressing up as an old man for Halloween when I was in sixth grade—even smoked a plastic cigar. I remember feeling the most comfortable I ever had in clothes before that moment. I remember thinking, "I wish I could wear this all the time."

I've always liked ties. There was a short period of time in the 90's when they were in—at least somewhere—so I got away with them. I haven't worn them since. I put one on for a job interview the other day, a thin shiny army green one with little pale blue dots. With jeans, a pullover long sleeve t-shirt and some expensive wingtips. I felt just right.

Could it actually finally be time for me to feel at home in my own clothes? This would be such a life upgrade. For the majority of my life to date, unless I am wearing jeans and a white t-shirt, I feel distractingly consumed by what I have on, like I am trying to be something that I feel like I'm not, that somebody will see through me, see that what I have on is the world's most transparent, poorly compiled costume. The more girl clothes I wear, the more naked I feel.

THE GIRL FROM THE COFFEE SHOP

I ran into an actual gay woman I know in a coffee shop last night. Because I know only three or four gay women, and because I am apparently scared to death of lesbians and drawn only to straight women over and over again, I doubled back to chat with her before I left. I am trying to stretch myself. We sat and talked for a bit, and she asked me questions no one else has yet, freeing questions, questions that offered me answers just by virtue of their being asked. She told me she'd be my "welcome wagon," introduce me to the community. We left with plans to see each other again. I think it will be nice to have a friend on the inside.

THE BRUSH OFF

I had a conversation, my third, with yet another woman whose friendship I'd dropped because she was beautiful and my heart wanted to lean toward her. I walked right up to her after years of passing here and there through town and said, "Got a minute?"

We stood near the school, and I told her how it is and how it was, apologized for the brush off, gave a real apology for my coolness, like the kind you offer after you realize you've been drunk and hurting people for years.

She said "I accept your apology," and too she said some kind, honest things like "What you're doing is the most important thing you could do for your girl." I took that one in, "What else can we do for our girls but show them how to live authentically?"

I thanked her for that. I'm putting it down here so I remember she said it without my even baiting her. These short, real talks feel like necessary work, like setting records straight and clearing the brush off of old paths. I step into them when they appear one at a time, with a goal for all the ways before me cleared.

WHAT WE SAID #8

My husband is researching DIY divorce now, reminding me I need to get work, any work, and also both thanking me when I cook dinner and articulating his anger like he's never been able to before. We are up to our necks in the painful clarity of what really is, somehow intermittently tender and stiff as we keep living in this house, waiting for the next things to come.

DOG SUIT

I called my older brother yesterday. I told him I'm gay and then asked to borrow six thousand dollars, all within the span of about 40 seconds. He said he wanted to give me the money after only a couple more beats. I called him because the electricity was about to be shut off in our house, and too because I know it's time for me to launch from here now, even if my husband won't yet. I hope this is bravery and not anything else that's masking as bravery.

My brother called me back later and explained exactly how he was going to pull off getting the money to me, like we were buying something we both wanted. I told him I'd known he would say yes to me in exactly the way that he did. Then we talked about what's really going on. And at some point in my telling I said, "It's hard to be a person treated like an issue."

It expressed the core of a thing I've been thinking on these past months. I keep saying when people ask me how I'm doing:

"The friends part. The hardest part is the friends part—harder than telling my boys, harder than living alongside my husband. It's the friends part that's knocked me off."

And it has. I keep saying that I understand intellectually why my dearest friends have responded the way they have—a couple in sad, disappointed, angry fear, a few more in sad, paralyzed, quiet fear. The two who are saddest and maddest have me perplexed. I am angry about their responses finally, still a little stunned and foggy when I think of them, but more angry than before, more indignant, though I don't feel the energy of that emotion, just the head-shaking stupor of it.

Twenty five years of friendship, and somehow this move in my life has them not able to see me at all. They see the issue of homosexuality when they look at me. It is like a tall opaque wall they are unwilling to scale, a wall that leaves them lobbing opinions and feelings over the top to try to reach me. They don't see me, not anymore. It's the not-being-seen that hurts most of all. Even if I understand, it's the hurt. I am struck by how powerful their ideas are to them, so powerful that I have somehow become un-see-able to them, like I'm dressed up in a dog suit now and nobody is even trying to peer into the mouth hole to figure out who's in there.

BUTT DIALS

I woke up today with a clearer sense of the small, confusing advances that keep coming my way from the girl who I thought liked me but didn't. The kissing emojis and the real looks she sends me now—they are like accidental phone calls, butt dials, the unintended pressing of a button, the ones you receive that pop up a name you would love to connect with but who you know never meant to call.

They are the calls you know not to answer, and not to return. You don't return butt dials.

GAY CREDO

Yesterday's outgoing early morning prayer: *You are my provider.* And incoming immediately: *Let's get you snug.*

There was a lovely booze and fries outing to a seaside spot with a girl I went to the movies with last week. The one who I've been texting with, the one from the coffee shop who seemed like a friend. We'd sat at the movies and I felt myself sitting in my movie seat next to her and leaning in her direction without even planning to, like my body knew something I hadn't yet figured out. I just kept leaning.

Also, there was a talk with my husband that left us both our own sorts of teary.

There was a twenty dollar cash deposit on a place of my own too—my last free twenty handed over to the nice teacher who owns the studio in the block behind mine, a declaration of living there, the girl from the coffee shop standing beside me as I handed it over.

And now I'm sitting on my balcony with a morning cigarette and the last of the coffee pot, sketching where to put my furniture in my one-room house, already dressed as me: dream wingtips and a vintage tie I've been waiting for my boys to wear for years, setting it aside every time they put it in the pile of clothes they'd never wear when we'd clean through their dressers culling for the stuff they'd outgrown.

I keep telling the people who ask me how I am that I breathe into a high space in my chest now, a place that hasn't had any real air in it for a long time, not since I used to sit in blanket forts in the backyard of the house we lived in for a while when I was eleven.

Today I will take more resumes to more places I never thought I'd work: hotels, retail shops, places that give paychecks. Today I will bring a few things up to the studio—a rug I made, some sheets for the bed, and probably one of my sewing machines. And I will make lists of what else needs to come.

I hear Lisa the therapist's voice in my head, "What do you know today?"

Today I don't know much of what's ahead, well, nothing of what's ahead. But I know this—I know what I believe. And I believed it all before I ever began looking for love, before I ever asked myself if I was gay, before I ever asked Lisa the Therapist the question, "How gay do you have to be to be gay," before I knew whether I'd be brave enough to hear the answer:

I believe in comfortable underpants.

I believe in riding bikes.

I believe in seven year olds and the power of noodles to fix anything.

I believe in red punch and saltine crackers on a napkin.

I believe in casseroles.

I believe in stories.

I believe in Love.

And now I add one more to the list: I believe in gays.

EPILOGUE

I go to the ice plant when the chance comes and the ocean waves greet me with their forever change and constancy. I breathe still into that higher place in my chest. And I want to live and do this life, no more wishing I could die, no more carrying a deep ball of sadness around in my gut as I go, no more holding all the sadnesses around me my own.

I married the girl, the one from the coffee shop, and we have built a family with this full set of five children between us. I have seen my wife turn out to be exactly who I saw her to be on that day when we kissed for the first time: warm, steady, unflinching in kindness, ready to see me and allow me to see her.

I watched my husband re-marry and saw him float away on the tide of his unknowing how to still love me. I have watched my children in pain and still finding their feet. I have watched their beautiful souls grow in spite of and in light of their steady connection to me. I have every month felt more of their struggle inside my own as my capacity for love has unshaken itself from the terror and upset of coming out. I have been re-given friendships that I lost, received important apologies and have had forgiveness handed through me like a flash of light, beyond my control and freely given, as happens in response to true apologies. I've had the consoling experience of seeing old friends love my new life. I have what I need in my life, all of my dear ones beside me.

I still believe deeply that God is real, that he spoke to me, that he walked beside me, that I was in fact, Abednego or one of his brothers, shielded from the flames of the life that lit up around me. And I still haven't figured out how to express that faith, where to take it. I still hear my prayers more than I say them. But I am leaning in on that, listening to more and more people of faith who strike me as trustworthy and true-hearted, people who echo an incoming prayer I received a bit ago, a sort of summary line from God himself: *You get to do your life. I get to love you.*

Our stories don't stop, of course, but they don't kill us. Even the ones we think will take us out completely can't stand up to the way God keeps our knees from buckling, offers us the unexpected gift of survival. Wants more than anything, it seems to me, to give us life. And I will go now, and I will live it.

ACKNOWLEDGMENTS

Thank you to Stephen F. Austin State University Press for taking mine off the stack. And to my writing group for waiting until now to kick me out of the boat.

Special thanks to the friends who have walked with me through all of the drafts and all of the iterations of this book--and my life. Both have see significant revision in seven years. Thanks to my family. I'll never know how I got so lucky.

Most of all, thanks to Christi: For being unafraid of the architecture of my particular soul. And for finding the note that I wrote.

CPSIA information can be obtained
at www.ICGtesting.com
Printed in the USA
BVHW050158140822
644510BV00005B/12